The Fogg Family of America

A. J. Fogg, J.L.M. Willis

BIBLIOLIFE

The Fogg Family of America.

The Reunions of the Fogg Families, 1902-3-4-5-6.

ADDRESSES, POEMS, NEWSPAPER REPORTS AND MEMORIES.

Edited by
Mrs. A. J. Fogg and J. L. M. Willis, M. D.

" He who forgets his ancestors is like a stream without a source, a tree without a root."

Eliot. Maine.
Historical Press.
1907.

CONTENTS.

iii.

PREFACE.

There is a singular interest in family name and story. Successive generations leave their impress; we eagerly gather their records as treasures. Every new unfolding of the earlier homes, occupations and characteristics, we receive and register with carefulness, not only to aid our own memories, but to transmit them to those who shall succeed us.

We issue this folio for this reason. Its merit is, that it revives, perpetuates and familiarizes the early names, the old homesteads, the words, ways, and even the Puritan atmosphere.

Yet more,—it brings us, of to-day, into fellowship; and gives us the consciousness that we are descendants of the same ancient fireside and family.

These simple pages give the origin of our yearly reunions; and contain addresses of the assemblies.

They are printed as memorials of sessions too pleasant to glide into a Forgotten Past.

Origin of the Fogg Reunions.

In November, 1900, Mrs. Adna J. Fogg began to gather data for a memorial of the Foggs in the United States.— In her correspondence with those of the name, she suggested that a *Reunion* be held at an early date.

In September, 1901, Mrs Fogg, her husband and son, called at Bride Hill, Hampton, N. H., the home of Mr. John H Fogg. In her earnest conversation with him, it was determined to have the gathering of the Foggs in the following year,—1902, Sept. 2,—which would be the Golden Wedding Day of the said John H. Fogg.

Not only was a *Call* issued and mailed to every known Fogg address, but Mrs Fogg also inserted it in her Genealogical circular. The happy result was that one hundred and ninety-three descendants of SAMUEL FOGG, the original settler, assembled to honor his memory in the town where his earliest American home was established.

THE RECORD OF THE FIRST MEETING.

Fogg Family, Sept. 2 1902, Hampton Beach, N. H.

Sept 2, 1902, 11.30 o'clock, A. M. Louis Everett Fogg, Portsmouth, N. H., called the meeting to order. He stated the object of the assemblage :—

To form a Family Association, for the purpose of holding future meetings, and also to assist in collecting the names and dates for a Family Genealogy.

Willis Allen Fogg, of Malden, Mass , was temporary Chairman; and at his request, Mrs. Adna J. Fogg suggested the following names as the Officers of the Association for the First Year :

PRESIDENT : John Henry Fogg, Hampton, N. H

VICE PRES.: Willis Allen Fogg, Malden, Mass.
Rev. John Blake Fogg, Monmouth, Me.
Louis Everett Fogg, Portsmouth, N. H.
Rev. Charles Grant Fogg, Union, Ct.
Dr. John Smith Fogg, Biddeford, Me.

(next page·)

(Vice Presidents continued)

        Walter Raleigh Fogg, Columbus, Ohio.
        Dr Fred'k Sam'l Fogg, Roxbury, Ms.
        Orlando R. Fogg, Hancock, N. H.

TREASURER   Walter LeRoy Fogg, Portsmouth, N. H

AUDITOR: Frederick LeRoy Fogg, Augusta, Maine

EXECUTIVE COMMITTEE·

   George Osgood, Kensington, N. H
   Horace Tower Fogg, Norwell, Mass.
   Hiram Hayes Fogg, Bangor, Maine.
   Simon S Fogg, Hancock, N H
   Elmer Henry Fogg, Hartford, Ct
   George Ellery Fogg, Greene, Maine
   Adna J. Fogg, Boston, Mass
   Mrs George L Davenport. Cohasset, Mass
   Frank Appleton Fogg. Laconia Mass.
   Mrs Charles Gilmore Fogg, Providence, R. I
   Mrs. Ella Fogg Hasty Limerick, Maine
   Miss Bertha Grace Fogg, Lynn, Mass

Moved by Lewis Everett Fogg that with the addition of Mrs Adna J Fogg, as Secretary, the persons selected be unanimously elected ,

John Blake Fogg seconded the motion ;

and they were chosen to hold office until the next Annual Meeting

An invitation having been received from the President, —John Henry Fogg, and his estimable wife,—to visit them at their home, Bride Hill, the ancient Fogg homestead, where they were celebrating their Golden Wedding, more than one hundred Fogg descendants availed themselves of the opportunity ; a pleasant half hour was spent in tracing the premises, and in listening to remarks by the Rev. John Blake Fogg

The company returned to the Beach, and dinner was served at the Ocean House

The session was then called to order by the Chairman, Lewis Everett Fogg   An interesting paper on "The Influence of Genealogy," by G. M Shedd, of Nashua, N H (whose wife is of Fogg descent,) was read by the

Rev. Charles Grant Fogg, of Union, Conn., and much appreciated.

Additional remarks, pertinent to the occasion were made by Rev. John Blake Fogg, Rev. Charles Grant Fogg, and Adna J. Fogg.

Mrs. George L. Davenport, Cohasset, Mass., expressed the desire that the company should have more of these meetings.

Charles E. Fogg, Whitman, 'Mass., was preparing his line for the Fogg Memorial.

Rev. John Blake Fogg, Monmouth, Maine, was glad of the pleasing opportunity to meet so many agreeable people

Mrs. Catherine B. Fogg, Dorchester, Mass. the oldest lady present, being in her 81st year, thought it the duty of the entire family to assist Mrs. Fogg in her Genealogical investigations.

Reference was made to the Museum, of Harvard, erected in memory of William Hayes Fogg, of New York.

Members of the Executive Committee reported that the next Annual Meeting would be Thursday, the third week of August, 1903. Annual dues, fifty cents.

The following committee was appointed to aid in the compilation of the "Genealogical and Biographical Memorial of the Fogg Family in the United States :''

> Rev. Charles Grant Fogg, Union Conn.
> Hubbard Fogg, Sandford, Maine.
> Charles Richard Fogg, Newburyport, Mass.
> Mrs George L. Davenport, Cohasset, Mass
> Mrs. Horace Fogg, Greene, Maine.

Samuel James Fogg of Newburyport, Mass., was the oldest gentleman present.

The meeting adjourned till the call of the Secretary.

Charter Members.   1902.

George E Fogg, Greene, Maine.
Mrs. George E. Fogg,
Darwin C. Fogg, Keene, N. H.
Adna J- Fogg, Boston, Mass.
Mrs. Adna J Fogg, Boston, Mass.
Mrs. Susan F. Hill, Lynn, Mass.
Willis A. Fogg, Malden, Mass
Morris B. Rowe, Roxbury, Mass
Mrs. Morris B. Rowe,
Mrs. George W. Knapp, Providence, R. I.
Mrs. Mary Heath, Brookline, Mass.
Mrs. Phebe J. Twombly, Framingham, Mass.
Miss Alice Twombly, Framingham, Mass.
Mrs. D F Shedd, Haverhill, Mass.
Mrs. E. A. R. Ayres, East Boston, Mass
Mrs. A C. Hilliard. Lynn, Mass.
Rev. Charles E Fogg, Union, Ct.
Mrs Elisha A. Shedd, Nashua, N H
Mrs. J. C McGillivary, Chelsea, Mass.
Horace Fogg, Greene, Maine.
Mrs. Horace Fogg,
Lewis E Fogg, Portsmouth, N. H.
Mrs. Lewis E. Fogg,
Walter LeRoy Fogg, Portsmouth, N. H
Hastings Fogg, Meredith, N. H
Frank A Fogg, Laconia, N H
Mrs Frank A. Fogg,
George Osgood, Kensington, N. H.
Mrs George L Davenport, Cohasset, Mass.
Rev J. B. Fogg, Monmouth, Maine.
Charles A. Smith, Stratham, N. H.
Mrs. Charles A. Smith,
Almon H. Fogg, Houlton, Maine.
Dr John S Fogg, Biddeford, Maine.
Fred L. Fogg, Augusta, Maine

Genealogy and its Importance.

BY G. M. SHEDD

Read by the Rev. Charles Grant Fogg (See page two.)

I have been invited to say a few words on *Genealogy
and its Importance* In the first place let me say that I feel
greatly honored by the invitation ; and at the same time it
is with reluctance that I make the attempt to tell an
audience like this, of the importance of keeping a record
of their ancestors, and of the great benefit of it to their
posterity Your very presence here is evidence enough to
satisfy any one who is not prejudiced, that it is something
in which you all take more than a passing interest.

It was a remark of Edmund Burke, " They who never
look back to their ancestors, will never look forward to
their posterity " We wish to know who they were , when
and where they lived ; their toils, privation, suffering,—
for from them has been derived all that is peculiar to our
New England homes ; and from here the same influences
that have gone out to other sections of our country, bear
fruit of the early teachings of our ancestors. Is it, therefore, any wonder that they should desire to learn from
whence these peculiar ideas sprang, that have been the
key-note to the success of many who can trace their ancestors to the first or early settlers of New England ?

Among them are the descendents of SAMUEL FOGG,
ancestor of the Fogg families ; and, as you all may know,
one of the early settlers of this town.

Two hundred and eighty-four years have passed since
that day, and we are gathered here on the shore of the
Atlantic, coming from every point of the compass, almost
from the shores of the Pacific. Why do we gather here ?
That we may become better acquainted with each other,
and so learn more of the history of our ancestors as well
as of each other. Here is where the importance of
Genealogy comes in Had no records been kept, we would
not be assembled here today. Eight generations are too
many for the story to be handed down from generation to
generation by word of mouth, scattered as you are from
the Atlantic to the Pacific.

No doubt many of you have seen the time when you wished to know who were your ancestors farther back than your great grandfather ; and if he were the first of the family who came over? That was my experience when a boy It took years to learn who was the immigrant ancestor of the family, which I now trace to the year 1642. Had no record been kept, I would never have been able to learn about them earlier than 1753 , as no Genealogical Record of the family, earlier than that, had been kept What has been gathered previous to that date, is from the colonial records, town and church registers, and in many instances having to resort to burial places where their ashes rest, and the time worn stones tell the tale

This should be evidence enough of the importance of a Genealogical Record being kept in each family ; and I trust the time is come when its importance is felt as never before

Words of mine may not make the strongest impression of the great importance of keeping a Family Record ; but should anyone here have a desire to obtain a more lasting impression, let him undertake the task of compiling a Genealogy of several generations, and I will guarantee they will quickly perceive the importance of a family record

I will not weary you by citing cases where fortunes have been at stake, and many are now trying to trace their ancestors for the evidence that they are lineal descendants of some one who has left an estate to which there is no record of the nearest relative. This, if nothing else, should be a motive, but not the only one

Much early history and general information is gained in looking up the Genealogy of a family. It will be the greatest surprise of your life, if once undertaken Trace it far enough and you may find that your next door neighbor is connected with you in the early times This was my own experience, never dreaming of such relationship. In searching old records, I found that the immigrant ancestors,—my neighbor's and my own,—signed a petition in 1645, for a grant of land in Massachusetts.

Following up the line farther, I found more than thirty of my neighbor's ancestors had married mine.

The Fogg ancestors came from England; and in a sermon, preached by the Rev. William Hyde, in Weymouth,
Mass , he traces the ancestry of King Edward VII, back
to the line of David of old So who knows but the Foggs
might trace their line back to the same origin, if they had
only seen the importance of a Genealogical Record in
earlier days¹

I also read the other day, that Queen Elisabeth had the
chart or tree made of her line ; tracing the same back to
Adam and Eve I suppose we all claim that we are their
descendants; so all we lack is the one important thing —
a Genealogical Record of the same !

Fogg Family. Second Reunion.

AUGUST 20, 1903. HAMPTON BEACH, N. H.

The Second Annual Reunion of the Fogg Family
Association of America, met at the Casino, Hampton
Beach, N. H Thursday, August 20, 1903, at 11 o'clock
Bert P. Doe, Newfield, N H. Secretary pro tem.

The meeting was called to order by the President, John
Henry Fogg, of Hampton   To this gentleman belongs
the honor of living on the ancestral acres which were
cleared and cultivated by Samuel Fogg the orginal settler,
and which for more than two-hundred and fifty years have
been handed down from sire to son,—eight generations.

The " Greeting Song," composed by C. E Pollock, was
sung . Mrs. Louis E. Fogg, of Portsmouth, pianist

The Rev John Blake Fogg, led in prayer.

The Address of Welcome, by the First Vice President,
Willis A. Fogg, had its interesting historical allusions —

Address of Welcome

WILLIS A FOGG

I have been requested to offer a few words of welcome
in behalf of our worthy President of the Association   We
all regret that he has chosen a substitute

It gives me great pleasure to greet so many noble sons
and daughters of our forefather ; and to extend to all a
most hearty welcome to this our Second Reunion of the
Fogg Family in America

Today nature unites with the achievements of a prosper-
ous nation in words of welcome.

At this season of the year the spirit of welcome is borne
along by the summer breeze, while the sound waves
vibrate with the exercises of Old Home Week   We are
welcomed to the arms of the broad ocean, extending from
our feet outward to England, the land of our forefathers.

In this busy world of ours, we do well to turn aside

from our usual avocations, to study and contemplate the subject of our early family history.

From a patriotic point of view, the town of Hampton holds a warm place in our hearts, it being the home of our early parents, and located in the Granite State where the idea of Old Home Week had its birth.

Today we see the families again united ; the parents greeting their children, back from the city to the old home, there to live over again the scenes of childhood. We renew old acquaintances and return to our homes, glad to have had our opportunity to enjoy the Old Home Week and the family reunion.

It was a happy inspiration that prompted Mr. and Mrs. Adna J. Fogg to take action leading to this reunion. We owe to them our heartfelt gratitude and appreciation for their services rendered in compiling history relating to our family, and in the many ways in which they have labored to make this event a success.

One has said : '' It is a noble faculty of our nature to be able to connect our thoughts, our sympathies and our happiness, with what is far distant in place or time, and looking before and after to hold communion at once with our ancestors and our posterity.''

When we contemplate the early history of this country, we find many worthy names who shared the hardships and dangers that menaced them on all sides while engaged in providing food and shelter for their families They solved the problems that arose from time to time, in a creditable manner, considering their limitations. Their trust being in God, they feared no danger.

In the history of this town, the name of Fogg appears often in connection with the Indian wars ; and once in the war of 1812. Later on, I am told, seventy-five engaged in the Civil War.

We honor our early forefathers for the sacrifices they made in order to bequeath to us a land of freedom and prosperity.

We admire their courage and devotion to religious liberty, that impelled them to break away from their old association in their native land, and sail away across the sea, to enter npon a new life in this then an unknown wilderness.

When we consider the toils, trials, sufferings and sorrows that the people had to encounter, we congratulate ourselves that we had our birth in this period of our nations history ; a country marvellously developed in all that pertains to educations and inventions ; possessing unlimited resources, enabling us to compete in all markets of the world

The ocean, lakes and rivers, in connection with the great railroad systems, afford the necessary avenues to carry the millions of passengers every year , and to transport the products of a productive soil, yielding bountiful crops of cotton, wheat, corn, and other farm products, in the numerous steamships that are plying day and night between our ports.

While stowed in the bowels of the earth are immense quantities of. coal, iron, and an ample supply of gold, silver, copper, lead and tin ore,—which, added to the wealth of our forests in timber and valuable wood, makes us a self-supporting people

It is a precious heritage that is handed over to our keeping. May we give good account of our stewardship ; and render faithful service to our city or town in which we reside.

In the exercises pertaining to this occasion, I hope we shall all heartily unite, and in this manner deepen our friendships and awaken a keener interest in the subject of good government in this the leading nation of the world

When we separate may we be led to exclaim with Whittier : —

    So then beach, cliff, and wave farewell ;
    We bear no token stone or glittering shell ;
    But long and oft shall memory tell
      Of this thoughtful hour musing by the sea

The address of the Vice President was followed by a vocal selection, full of melody, by Miss Charlotte Bean, of Walpole, Mass

A very interesting paper on the earliest emigrant of the family and the earliest days in New England next claimed the attention and thought ·

Samuel Fogg and the Early Foggs.

BY DR JOHN SMITH FOGG, Biddeford, Me

Read by Elmer H Fogg of Hartford, Ct.

Some people of the United States consider themselves too democratic and free to bother their minds about their ancestry That is their common excuse , yet the fact remains that these same people, who so decry the time-honored custom of keeping genealogical lines straight, are the very people who find it impossible to refer to accurate data of the birthdays of their own parents and grand-parents ; and to whom a lineal tracing of seven or eight generations of their family, would be more intricate than they would care to divulge in print

It is quite common to hear a person say that his name is of English, Scotch, Welsh, or other origin ; and it is also very easy for such a person to carelessly mention the fact that his American ancestor was one of three brothers who came over a century or two ago But for such a person to prove his descent is another matter entirely ; and it is in the proof of one's descent that a certain amount of pride is taken ; for such proof reveals the character and honesty of ancestors who, having lived a God-fearing and sterling life, have their names, and the names of their children and children's children, indelibly preserved in the records of church, province and state

So common has the remark been that an ancestor was one of three brothers who came over many years ago, that it apparently looks as if every family who sent emigrants from the Old World to America, always sent three of their sons. But there are no authentic records which show that three Fogg brothers came to America together. Nor can all by the name of Fogg claim descent from the first Fogg who landed here; for there are a few in the United States whose ancestors did not come over from England until the Nineteenth Century, but so early in the century that they escaped being classed among our immigrants who came

over here in steamships. There are a very few others
from Denmark, who are the representatives of the original
Danish family ; for the name of Fogg was known in the
land of the Vikings before it was known in England. It
is one of the oldest names ; and antedates the history of
England There is reason to believe that the name was
well known in Italy during the height of the Roman
Empire, and the Danes by the name of Fogg, probably
represent a branch older than our own English, Welsh,
or Norman branches

The first by the name of Fogg in America, of whom we
have authentic history, came to the shores of Massachusetts, from England, two hundred and seventy-three years
ago ; and of them we have official records since 1630.

Before proceeding any further with the name of Fogg,
it is but just to those who first came to this country, to
give their reason for leaving England :

On the third of November, 1620, King James of England, signed a patent by which the adventurers of the
northern colony of Virginia between 40 degrees and 48
degrees North were incorporated as the Council established
at Plymouth, in the County of Devon, for the planting,
ruling, ordering and governing of New England in
America. This was the great civil basis of the future
patents and plantations that divide this country.

This Council, by a deed indented under the common
seal, and bearing date, March 27, 1627, did bargain and
sell unto some knights and gentlemen about Dorchester,
that part of New England that lies between the Merrimac
and Charles rivers These gentlemen were brought into
acqaintance with several other religious persons of like
quality in and around London, who, being at first associated with them, at last bought of them all their right and
interest in that part of New England before mentioned,
Their purpose in buying was to settle some plantation in
New England on account of religion, and where such as
were called Non-conformists might, with the favor and
leave of the King, have a place of reception if they should
transport themselves unto America, and there to enjoy the
liberty of their own persuasion in matters of worship and

church discipline without disturbance of the peace of the
Kingdom, and without offence to others not like-minded
with themselves.

The King confirmed unto these gentlemen a new grant
of all the land mentioned ; and in 1628 the company sent
over agents to look after their interests, and to make way
for the settling of another colony in Massachusets. —
Previous to this nothing had been done of any moment by
the settlers in Massachusetts, except fishing and trading.

At a General Court, held in England by the Company,
August 28, 1629, it was considered to settle the government of the Company in New England.   An adjournment
was made to the next day at seven o'clock, when arguments were to be heard until nine o'clock ; and at the
latter hour, which is the hour appointed for the meeting
of a General Court, a vote was to be taken on the question
of removal   At that hour, August 29, 1629, it was voted
that the government and patents should be removed to
New England

Such a transaction stands alone in the history of English
colonization   It was a bold move, but the men consti-
tuting that Court were bold men.   The power of that
Court to transfer the seat of their government, has been
seriously doubted, and even denied ; and it is evident from
their charter that the Corporation was to remain in England like that of the East India Company, or other great
companies, with power to settle plantations within the
territory under such forms of government and magistracy
as should be fit and necessary

The boldness of the step is not more striking than the
silent acquiescence of the King in permitting it to take
place   That the Company's action met with opposition
from some quarter, is evidenced when, on Sept 29, 1629,
the Company deemed it expedient "to take advice of
learned counsel," whether their step was legal or not —
The advice of the "learned counsel" of that day is now
seen to have been in favor of the action , and it is due to
his advice that the first government in New England was
established

October 20, 1629, Mr. John Winhtrop was unanimously
chosen Governor for the ensuing year; and immediately
took steps to prepare his fleet for departure from England
the following Spring.

Historical writers have repeatedly commented on the
courage and hardihood of these persons of rank and good
circumstances in life bidding a final good-by to their native
country of England, with all its delights and conveniences,
and exposing themselves, their wives and their children to
the inevitable hardships and sufferings in a long voyage
across the Atlantic, which, in those days, consumed two
months or more.   Their destination was a most inhospit-
able shore, destitute of any kind of buildings to secure
them from the inclemency of the weather, and not possessing any of the food to which they had been accustomed in
their former home.   Nor were their hearts buoyed by the
reports which the agents of the Company had sent home
In lieu of praise of the new country in which they had
lived for a year, their reports had been of the most dis-
couraging character.   Their description of New England
could hardly coincide with our present opinion of its
fertile resources

A nobler body of men and women never left their native
soil to colonize a new land . and it was in reference to the
persecution and exile of these people that Milton wrote
in 1641 .—

"What numbers of faithful and freeborn Englishmen
and good Christians have been constrained to leave their
home, their kindred and friends, and whom nothing but
the wide ocean and the savage deserts of America could
hide and shelter from the fury of the bishops
I shall believe there cannot be a more ill-boding sign to
a nation,—God turn the omen from us,—than when the
inhabitants, to avoid insufferable grievances at home, are
enforced to forsake their native country "

Such were the reasons which caused our progenitors to
emigrate from England ; and that those by the name of
Fogg are thoroughly independent in their views in
Church and State matters, is easily proven in history.—
And it is somewhat surprising that only *two* by the name

of Fogg rebelled against a religion distasteful to them, and came to America. But it would be none the less surprising to know that rhe Foggs remaining in England, were equally emphatic and true to any cause or religion they espoused there.

The name of FOGG in England is of the greatest age. Its antiquity is interesting, and its nationality almost perplexing. It is English as far as the history of England goes: and it is Danish, and Welsh, and Norman. It is found in that finest national record of Europe, the Domesday Book, compiled by commissioners appointed by William the Conqueror, in 1086 ; and the Foggs are found as land owners in the *Rotula Hundredorum*, or Hundred Rolls, prepared in 1273, by King Edward I, on his return from Palestine.

The Foggs in America of English descent, are as English as England is in herself. The name of Fogg was known in Denmark before English was spoken in England, and the Danes of that period were the Jutes, who held that part of the peninsula now called Denmark.

When the Northmen in their black piratical crafts, seized the northern part of France and settled it, the Fogg blood was among them ; and later allied itself to some of the noblest blood in France.

Kent County in England is the most solid part of England. It is the England of the English ; and here the Fogg family took its firmest hold,—owning vast estates in this country nearly a thousand years ago, and helped shape the destiny of England.

Picture to yourself one of the earliest Foggs. He was of the tribe of Jutes who inhabited what is now Denmark. The other two tribes who afterwards invaded what is now England, were from the Schleswig-Holstein provinces of Germany. Possibly this Fogg we see now was a North-man, and took part in the Norman Conquest; and may have fought his own blood which had preceded him in England. He was fair haired, blue eyed, big boned, and muscular. He probably had a store of unwasted vigor, an immense and almost brutal energy, an enormous and

unspent capacity for life, for feeling, for thought and for
action   He had an instinct for law and for freedom, a
splendid seriousness, a reverence for life and death. Such
is the description of a Viking; and in spite of their joy of
battle, their desire to feast, their drunken revelry, there is
a persistent undertone of melancholy.

The early home of the Jute, was a land of cold, harsh,
gloomy privations. but it was a land to breed real men !
It had dismal curtains of mist, miles of tangled forests
soaked and dripping with frequent rains, and their land
was frequently inundated by the fury of the sea.   The
land of these people descended to the eldest son.   The
younger sons took to warships ; and the high-prowed
galleys of the Vikings were a menace to the southern
countries

The Danish Foggs at present, are probably descendants
of the eldest sons of those by the name of Fogg in the
Jute tribes   And the descendants of Samuel Fogg, and
other English Foggs, have the blood of the younger sons
who settled in England and France   Who knows but the
Fogg blood was with the Northmen when they landed in
Massachusetts five hundred years before Columbus discovered America ?

Compare Pancoast's pen picture of a Northman, given
in synopsis above, with a New England Fogg, and you
will find the same ruggedness of anatomy and seriousness
of thought which was bred hundreds of years ago, and
which Samuel Fogg brought and bred in what is now
Hampton, New Hampshire. It was this healthful ruggedness that has made the Fogg family lasting through so
many generations, and kept the name for hundreds of
years, and which has produced an inate diplomacy from
mere strength of the character which former generations
have unconsciously instilled

As an example of this diplomacy, the life of Catharine
Parr will serve to illustrate   Everyone knows about this
Queen consort of King Henry VIII , but all by the name
of Fogg do not know her ancestry: Her grandmother
was Lady Jane Fogg, who was married at fourteen years
of age   Catherine Parr was great grandaughter of Sir
John Fogg of Ashford, great great grand daughter of

Sir William Fogg, of Repton, great-great-great grand daughter of Sir Thomas Fogg of Canterbury , and so on through a long line of Foggs

At the age of fifteen, Catharine Parr married Lord Burgh. Her second husband was Lord Latimer Her third husband was King Henry VIII, whom she married in great state at Hampton Court Palace, July 12, 1543. King Henry died in 1547 , and thirty-four days after his death, she married Lord Seymour of Sudley, uncle to King Edward VI.

Catharine Parr had the blood of Fogg in her veins, and she was the most diplomatic woman during the reign of Henry VIII, as she not only escaped the fate of the other wives, but actually ruled England while she was the Queen, and prevented many of the bad moves for which King Henry VIII was noted.

There are many instances in English history where Fogg blood has been high in official positions in both Church and State ; and their carved monuments and parchment records are still shown in England.

In connection with the name of Fogg in early New England, it will be necessary to mention the name of one of whom there is, at present, no authentic history known other than a few official data, and that is—JAMES FOGG,— who was known to be one of the eighty-two settlers of Gloucester, Massachusetts, who were proprietors of soil in 1650 There is no compiled history of him or his descendants. if he had any. His name is mentioned here with the hope that it will serve as a nucleus to further search.

The name of RALPH FOGG, of Salem, has been mentioned in the most cursory way by Fogg genealogists, and it has been due entirely to their lack of application, that a better history of him is not extant ; for the official records of Ralph Fogg are many in the archives of Massachusetts. As his name is frequently mentioned in connection with that of Samuel Fogg, it will be entirely appropriate for this page to contain a sketch of his life in New England, that it may serve as an incentive to the Fogg of the present day to hunt up old records, and make transcripts from official data, in order to find out if any of his descendants remained in America after 1675. At the present date it is not known ; but unknown mines of knowledge are constantly opening to the amateur genealogist. Records not seen today may spring into view to-morrow

According to the records of the Plymouth Colony, published by authority of the Massachusetts Legislature, Ralph Fogg came originally to Plymouth where he was admitted as a freeman, and had lands granted to him in 1633, and was taxed in 1634

From Plymouth he moved to Massachusetts Bay ; was made a freeman of the latter colony, September 3, 1634 He joined the First Church in Salem, as early as 1636. He was elected Treasurer in 1637   The office of treasurer was not confined to the town, but appears to have been co-extensive with the jurisdictional territory of the Salem Court.

He was Clerk of the quarterly sessions of the General Court, and, strange as it may seem, was High Sheriff at the same time, and discharged the dual duties of these offices for many years. He was the recorder for all the surveys made ; and was the first incumbent for Salem, of the office of Clerk of Writs, established December 10, 1641. In 1644. he was a member of the Artillery Company

In 1647. political dissentions arose in Salem. The enemies of Fogg, composed entirely of men upon whom he had served processes of law as High Sheriff. attempted to malign him by charging malfeasance of office He vigorously defended himself before church and council, and unhesitatingly rated the Governor,—who was then Endicott, declaring in a Church meeting, that the Governor was "both Judge and Jury '' For thus desecrating the Lord's Day, he was fined a few shillings by the church. But with all the autocratic powers of Governor Endicott, he evidently had fear of Ralph Fogg's knowledge of the inside mechanism of the General Court ; for the latter person received no worse sentence than to wear a piece of paper in his hat for two hours He diplomatically expressed regret that he had criticised the Governor on the Sabbath Day, and the paper sentence was not carried out.

His views regarding real justice in Salem and vicinity, can now be seen were correct. when we consider the ignorance displayed in Salem during the witchcraft days.

The remarkable daring of Ralph Fogg to publicly pro-
claim his views in the face of attacks from those upon
whom he had levied as Sheriff, and the apparent fear and
consequent dislike of him by Governor Endicott, was
more than commendable , for it was the stolid rashness of
right, for which he unhesitatingly stood up, and from
behind which he unmercifully scored his opponents with
his scholarly satire

Though living in Salem and owning large tracts of
land, neither the well known bigotry of some of the
inhabitants, nor the enmity of the Governor affected his
social status or deprived him of his lands ; and after
remaining in Salem a few years, he returned to England.
His two sons, who remained in America, were subjected
to many inconveniences after their father left, as they did
not have the benefit of his power and knowledge of colonial
affairs   One, David commander of a ship plying between
Barbadoes and New England, died ; the other, it is presumed, returned to England. Both sons were Quakers :
and the persecution of Quakers in Salem at that time
should be perpetuated by the erection of a monument in
Salem ; that the generation of today and future generations may be reminded of the former bigotry of a people,
who not only harrassed Quakers, but were known to
actually believe in witches

The site of Ralph Fogg's home in Salem, is now occupied by a street railway station, and around this he owned
several acres, besides large tracts elsewhere. These lands
he still held after his return to England, where he located
first at Plymouth and later in London, in the discharge of
his duties as a stockholder of a corporation established for
carrying on a trade in furs.

He died in London, March 15, 1673, and in his will
provides for his widow, Susanna, and three sons · John,
gentleman, of Barnstable, Devon, England ; David and
Ezekiel of New England

John and his mother came to New England, after the
death of Ralph Fogg, and remained to settle the estate,
and then returned to England   The Salem property was
sold, and was subsequently occupied by the houses of
John Milk, William Lake, William Longstaff, John
Hawthorne and others.

Ralph Fogg was a beautiful penman; and his official records on file at this day, are in striking and pleasing contrast to the ordinary ancient records. The first *Will* ever presented in the Essex County Court, is now in the Court files, folded and neatly endorsed by Fogg, in June, 1640.

So far as is known, Ralph Fogg was the first person in America who used a system of stenography. As the Clerk of the General Court, he used a system of characters similar to those of Thomas Archisden, of England : and Mr. Edward Howe, writing to John Winthrop, jr , in 1632, said : " These characters are approved in Cambridge to be the best yet invented ; and they are not yet printed or common "

To be the pioneer of stenography in America, is no small distinction for Ralph Fogg, when one considers the thousands of people now employed in that work, and the enormous saving of time, labor and money, by the aid of shorthand.

The names of James, Ralph, David and Ezekiel Fogg have now been mentioned in this paper as amongst the first settlers in New England But beyond the date of 1675, there are no known records of them or of any of their descendants

But—there was one Fogg in New England at that time, who was the progenitor of most of those by that name in America , and he was—

SAMUEL FOGG, who settled in *Hampton*, *N H.*
It is his history which will interest us most at this time, for we can stand upon the land and within sight of the broad acres which he owned and occupied more than two hundred and fifty years ago, and which now represents the ancestral home of the Fogg Family of America.

Let it be known to all by the name of Fogg, and to all descendants of a Fogg, that since this land was first occupied by Samuel Fogg to the present day, a period of more than two and a half centuries, it has never been conveyed by deed, but has been handed down from father to youngest son through many generations.

It has been mentioned that the land of the Northmen

bred real men. So with our own New England; for she has bred real men, and women too, who wrested a plenty from the tangled wastes of her forests and the bleak desolation of her shores.

Picture to yourself Samuel Fogg in his Puritanical garb coming to Boston about 1630, from Exeter, England.— Books on American ancestry tell us that he came over with that noble pioneer, John Winthrop, who was the first Governor of Massachusetts Bay Colony. Think for a moment of the little ship, Arabella, formerly the Eagle, but named the Arabella in honor of Lady Arabella Johnson, sister to the Earl of Lincoln, who accompanied her husband, Isaac Johnson, to America. This ship left Yarmouth, April 8, 1630, and arrived in Salem, June 12th, thus occupying over two months in a voyage that can now be made in less than a week.

Whether Samuel Fogg arrived in the Arabella or some other ship of Winthrop's fleet, cannot be stated in this paper. The exact lists of passengers are only in the Custom House records of England; no copies of them have ever been brought to this country. Let us assume, however, that he landed in Salem or Charlestown; or, possibly, Nantasket; for one of the seventeen ships, the Mary and John, landed there May 30, 1630.

Samuel Fogg's first view of the land where Boston now stands, revealed three small mountains; and the locality at that time was called Tri-mountain; a name perpetuated in the well-known Tremont street of today. The three mountains were where Pemberton Square, Louisbourg Square and Beacon Hill now are. The latter was originally called the Sentry, as on its top a pitch barrel was fixed, to be lighted as an alarm to the inhabitants, in case of invasion by the Indians. This beacon was blown down in November, 1789.

When the English first saw the three contiguous hills, they called the locality Tri-mountain; but the Indians had always called the place Shawmut; and to this day we have Shawmut Avenue, in memory of the Indian name. At a Court of Assistants held in Charlestown, Sept. 7, 1630, it was ordered that Tri-mountain be called Boston.

One may be pardoned for a certain amount of pride in the knowledge that the soil of Massachusetts was trodden by an ancestor even before the name of Boston was given to the city which we know by that name.

Samuel Fogg, however, did not remain in Massachusetts permanently, but went farther north, along the shore, and finally settled in Hampton, N. H , and his descendants have owned land along the New Hampshire coast and in York and Cumberland counties of Maine, for two and a half centuries

In Savage's Genealogical Dictionary of New England, it states that Sarah Currier, daughter of Richard Currier, of Salisbury, England, married June 23, 1659, Mr Samuel Fogg, of Hampton, N H This record is incorrect unless there were two by the name of Samuel Fogg living in Hampton at that time ; and there is no official statement that such was the case. Samuel Fogg, our progenitor, could not have married Sarah Currier in 1659, for his first wife was living at that time   She died in 1661, and a year later he married his second wife.

His first wife was Anne Shaw, of Hampton, whom he married, Oct 12, 1652, when he was 39 years of age. She died in 1661 . and she bore him four sons and one daughter Two of the sons and the daughter died in infancy ; but the eldest and the youngest children lived :—

Samuel, jr born in 1653 ;
Daniel, born April 16, 1660.

Samuel, jr , married Hannah Marston, Oct 19, 1676, when he was twenty-three years old He settled in Hampton on his father's estate ; and some of his descendants have always lived there.

Daniel, the youngest son, was less than a year old when his mother died after eleven years of wedded life ; and when he was two years old, his father,—Samuel, senior,— married as his second wife, Mary Page, daughter of Rob't Page, of Hampton. Her father was one of the prominent men of Hampton, a large landowner, and a member of the General Court. At the time of her marriage to Samuel Fogg, she was but nineteen years of age. and Samuel was forty-nine years of age, a widower, and with two children, one eleven and the other two years of age.

By this marriage, Mary (Page) Fogg bore her husband two sons and a daughter .

Seth and James,

Hannah ;

and these children have many descendants

The youngest son, Daniel, by the first wife, (Anne Shaw Fogg,) was brought up under the care of the second wife until he was twelve years of age. His father died at that period, and this youth was apprenticed to the blacksmith. He remained in Hampton until he was twenty-two, and then removed to the Spurwink river, in Scarboro, Me where he worked at his trade, and where he received several grants of land , and in 1684, at twenty-four years of age, he married Hannah Libbey, of Scarboro.

It is from this marriage that most of the Fogg descendants in York and Cumberland counties, in Maine, received their origin. There are also some of his descendants in Portsmouth and vicinity, as he removed his family from Scarboro to Portsmouth, in 1690, on account of the constant fighting of the Indians. His son, John, returned to Scarboro in later years, and located there permanently

There were a few colored people named Fogg, living in or near Portsmouth, in recent years. These are the descendants of the Fogg slaves, who took the name of their master, as was common at that time , and also common in the more recent ante-bellum days of the Southern States.

The settlement of Samuel's sons in Hampton and Scarboro, was the starting point of the third generation of those by the name of FOGG in this country Beyond this it will be needless to go in this paper, for each generative root continues to give its numerous branches that constantly multiply as the years approach recent times ; and each new born tendril has but served to more closely bind our allied interest in our common progenitor of Hampton.

As a lineal descendant of Samuel and Anne (Shaw) Fogg, in the eighth generation, through the youngest son Daniel and Hannah (Libbey) Fogg, it gives me pleasure to say that the Fogg family has helped in the moulding of the earliest history of this country. Let us try and cement our ties more closely by each contributing his mite of labor towards historical research. Let the Fogg Family remember that the blood of their ancestors stained the ground in Colonial Wars ; that during the Revolutionary War, Samuel Fogg's descendants were not inactive : for they were at Quebec, at Louisbourg, and wherever there there was hard exposure and risk of life In the Mexican War, and Civil War the red blood of the children of Samuel drenched the ground ; and in the Spanish-American War, and in opposing the armed resistance to the sovereignty of the United States in the Philipine Islands the descendants of Samuel Fogg did their duty to their country and to the memory of their grand old ancestor.

Let the present and coming generations remember these facts when reading the history of the United States, and have them serve as an incentive to the keeping of accurate and detailed family histories for the benefit of the Fogg of a hundred years hence.

Samuel Fogg, with the ruggedness of physique and the fighting qualities of his Northmen ancestors, hewed a home in the very heart of a New England wilderness, and it was his natural diplomacy and deep seriousness, that kept his life clean and free from the many temptations that beset a man in a new country

These qualities of restraint he inherited through the generations of the Fogg family who are entombed in Ashford and throughout England. Through the Sir John Fogg who was the intimate friend of King Edward III, the Black Prince ; or the Sir John Fogg to whom King Edwagd IV gave the manor Hathfield when he was comptroller of the King's household ; or the Sir John Fogg who, with King Edward III, Sir William Haute, Lord Scales, Earl Rivers, the Duchess of Bedford, all in their surcoats of arms, were perpetuated in a kneeling position in the great west windows of the cross aisle in the Church at Ashford

The colored glasses of the windows are gone ; and many of the Fogg tombs in England are so old that their carvings are worn almost smooth, but the carving of his home-tree in America by Samuel Fogg can never be erased, as each child born to his descendants will but represent a new figure to the memory of their ancestor.

Samuel Fogg lived his wiry, virile life for sixty years. His first child was born when he was forty years of age, and the last child when he was fifty-eight. His eldest son lived one hundred and seven years, his second son ninety-five years : his third son ninety years, and his fourth and last son ninety-two years.

These great ages in the second generation of the American strain of the Fogg blood from two wives, speak well for the healthy condition of Samuel Fogg ; and it is due to his perfect physical condition that we can look back with pride to the strong physical foundation he prepared as the sire of the many generations of the FOGG FAMILY IN AMERICA.

Ashael Fogg, of Lynn, Mass., followed the paper of Dr. J. S. Fogg, with not only forcible but with witty and humorous remarks on the question, " Do we Need a Genealogy ?"

An amusing story was next told by John H. Fogg, of Hampton ; followed by one from the Rev. John B. Fogg, of Monmouth, Maine.

Adjourned at one o'clock, for dinner.

Afternoon session, called to order at three o'clock, by the President.

Previous to this, a group picture of the assembly was taken on the steps of the Casino.

The President read the names of the following Officers, who were unanimously elected :

HONORARY PRESIDENT :
  John Henry Fogg. Hampton, N. H.

PRESIDENT: John Blake Fogg, Monmouth, Maine.

VICE PRES.: Lewis Everett Fogg, Portsmouth, N. H.
            Gridley R. Fogg, Skowhegan, Maine.
            George S. Fogg, Beverly, Mass.

SECRETARY and TREASURER :
  Mrs. Adna J. Fogg, Boston, Mass.

(next page.)

EXECUTIVE COMMITTEE:

Frank A. Fogg, Laconia, N. H.

Willis A. Fogg, Malden, Mass.

George Osgood, Kensington, N. H.

Mrs. Wayland I. Fogg, Lynn, Mass.

George E Fogg, Greene Corner, Maine.

Horatio Fogg Twombly, Framingham, Mass.

George O. Fogg, Winchester, Mass.

Nathaniel Conant, Brookline, Mass.

Mrs. Fred C. Browne, Portland, Maine.

A paper on the *Fogg Coat of Arms*, prepared by Charles Grant Fogg, of Frenchboro, Maine, was read by Mrs. Fred C. Brown, of Portland. It was listened to with great attention. (At the date of the address his residence was Union, Conn)

Heraldic Devices, Arms, &c.

REV. CHARLES GRANT FOGG

Read by Mrs Fred C Brown, of Portland.

Concerning Heraldic Devices and the Right of the Foggs in America to Bear the Arms of the Foggs of England :

Let us say at the outset, that only those who have engaged in historical research, can have any idea of the difficulties encountered   In obtaining ordinary historical data, the definite location of a needful fact, often requires months or years of patient labor, even when the parties are alive

Back of the second generation of actors, difficulties increase in geometrical ratio. Archives must be searched ; tombstone inscriptions copied,—when legible or in existence ; town records examined and parish registers transcribed. These last are the two most important means to New England genealogical data, and, alas! are the very ones often wanting. The early town records were often carelessly kept, and many have been lost.

Genealogical data, as such, is still more exacting.— Direct records must be had. Circumstantial evidence is absolutely of no use, except as clues for settling positively proved descent. A single break in the recorded chain, renders useless all previously acquired data, and nothing more can be done until the gap is filled.

The author of this paper has been following certain clues for over ten years, and has learned the chief rule of genealogical investigation. That rule is. *Take nothing for granted !*

A single instance shows the difficulties attending the tracing the descent of the New England families : The location of not a single grave of the Pilgrims who died that first terrible winter is known with certainty.

The connection of New England families with their European ancestors is yet more difficult to establish.— When that first, immigrant patriarch, and—to coin a word,—matriarch, have been definitely located, at once comes the query. '' From what place did they come?'' The ship on which each or both sailed, may be known ; but even then, at the port of embarkation, all trace may be lost

Assuming that they came from England, the only way is to begin with the most probable field, and examine the English parish registers. Usually those of a given family name will be found,. at last,*to have come from a certain definite region, or regions.

And here is where the science of *Heraldry* often proves of help If the name is a noble one, the investigator harks back to the noble line, and traces its branches and descendants, going to possible beginnings, and, genealogically, working backwards, from early dates to later.

Heraldry being an exact science, nothing more nor less than a pictorial statement of family name, descent and standing, it is the greatest aid to tracing the descent of those of noble blood.

So, in tracing New England ancestry, where it is desired to ascertain if the line is of noble blood, there are four stages, each of increasing difficulty :

First, local descent and connections

Second, tracing to the first immigrants

Third, the European home.

Fourth, the possible connection with a noble line.

This will explain the, as yet, partial success in the search

for a Fogg Coat of Arms Yet, we are on the track of
results.   As we shall later see, the name is of noble
English origin. It remains to be proved which of two or
three lines may be that of our first American, SAMUEL
FOGG, who is supposed to have come over "in one of the
six ships of John Winthrop."

Let it be understood that this search is undertaken in
the *historical* spirit. Especially is care taken to be accurate, and give only ascertained facts. In the preparation
of the Fogg genealogy, this question of possible noble
descent, with the accompanying coat of arms, came in as
a necessary factor in tracing the European origin of the
family.

Almost all the older New England families are descended from the English nobility, by some connection, often
being branches from younger sons who, taking the side of
the Puritans or Roundheads, came to America. Some are
of French Huguenot origin. By English, we include
Scotch and Irish, also Welsh.

It was the first intention, in giving this paper, to give
an illustrated sketch of Heraldry. But there is not time.
However, we will review a few fundamental facts, then
pass on to the family record.

Heraldry proper is not traced beyond the latter part of
the eleventh century.   *Heer*, army ; *Held*, champion ;
Blazen, to blow the horn

The important parts of the Coat of Arms, are the Field,
the Motto, and the Crest   The field tells the story of the
family descent, being the genealogical diagram, changing
as marriage combined various houses, effecting what was
practically a pictorial monogram. The shield was divided
into various parts, each telling its own story.

For a more detailed account, the best treatise the writer
has seen is *Heraldry Simplified*, by Frederick Curtis, published by the Dodge Publishing Co. New York.

To enlarge upon the finer points is, here, out of the
question. Enough to say that, to one versed in the science
and acquainted with the various family arms, a glance
would tell a person's descent, where the plan was carried
out. As if we should say,—"John Strong, second son of

William Strong, by his wife, Isabel DeCourcey, he the son
of the second William, she the daughter of Edonard
DeCourcey. It was very convenient, and, today, a knowledge of the science is essential to the historian, the story-
writer, or the traveller student.

The motto was the family watchword. It was sometimes changed, e g the head of the family in conquering
a rival, would sometimes take his motto. The crest was
placed above all. If a helmet, it showed valor on the
battlefield ; being usually represented with the visor down.
The number of bars, the color, or the plain helmet,
showed the rank of the owner These three divisions,
the Field, the Motto, the Crest, are the essentials ; and of
these, for the minute genealogist, the Field and the Crest.

During the reign of Henry III, in the thirteenth century,
a roll of arms, borne by the barons and knights of that
King, was formed. His successor, Edward I, in 1274,
ordained the compulsory use of arms and seals by his
coroners; and, later, ordained by statute that every freeholder should, at penalty of fine and amercement, have
his proper seal of arms

During the reign of Edward II, in 1307, a second roll of
arms was made, which comprised the names of 1160
persons.

Henry V, in 1413, prohibited, under heavy penalty, the
use of any arms to which the bearer was unable to show a
proper title, exception being made to those who had borne
a cognisance at Cressy, Poictiers, or Agincourt. In short,
as we would say, he forbade forgery.

During the 16th century, were appointed the Royal
Commissioners of Enquiry concerning the right to bear
arms. This commission, termed the *Heralds Visitation*,
attended different parts of the realm, and had the power to
summon all who bore or assumed arms, to produce their
credentials, and " To reprove, control and make infamous
by proclamation, all such as unlawfully and without
authority took such unto themselves."

Any one now able to prove descent from ancestors
acknowledged in these "visitations," is entitled to carry
his arms by right of inheritance ; or, failing that, from

some one whose right has been admitted. This is the
test, and is the one followed by the present writer in
examining data previous to the first part of the 17th
century.

In Ireland there was no thorough visitation. So. Ulster
King of Arms was empowered to give confirmation to all
who could prove their families had borne arms for several
generations.

We have now an idea of our limits. This means much.
So far as titles are concerned, the first Baronetcy was
instituted by James the First, in 1611. And in England
today, no existing title goes back of the 14th century.
Arms, of course, go much farther back.

Now as to the FOGGS. The writer grows more convinced
that the name is of Danish origin. In Denmark, a Fogh,
(note the spelling,) was ennobled in 1707 ; another in
1747. It has a Danish sound.   This origin, however,
remains to be proved.

The English records give the Coat of Arms of Sir
Thomas Fogge, of Danes Court, Tilmanster   Also are
given the Arms of Sir John Fogg, of Scots Hall

The late dates of the Danish nobles bar them from being
ancestors of the American branch of Fogg.   There is a
strong possibility that Sir John or Sir Thomas may be the
ancestor of our Hampton Samuel.

Burke's Peerage fails to show a Fogg title.   Therefore
the line has run out in England, and we must look farther
back for Arms.   Of course Sir John and Sir Thomas bore
Arms.   It also appears that Katherine Parr, who was
lucky enough to outlive her interesting husband, Henry
the 8th, was a Fogg in descent.   Of course she was of
noble blood, and came of arms-bearing stock.

The name has been traced back to the 13th century.
Was there a freeholder by the name of Fogg at that time ?
If so, he was obliged by Edward the First, to be labelled,
(for that was the exact idea,) with his own peculiar Seal
of Arms.   Is the name among the 1160 of Edward the
Second ?   This, the present writer cannot say ; nor has he
fully investigated the visitations.   But we have three
established points we may claim with reasonable certainty.

The case of Katherine Parr proves that, at the time of Henry the 8th, there must have been Fogg arms; she must have been of gentle blood. Also, Sir John and Sir Thomas bore arms.

The deduction is, that there have been accredited Arms to the Foggs of England. It has been ascertained,—the writer is informed upon good authority,—that the color of the Field of these Arms is gold ; the motto is, *Peradventure*. Now, the color is the feature that does not change. If these various Coats of Arms prove to have the same color, it will show considerable antiquity. This will require time to discover.

The only question remaining is, for us *the* one question, Was Samuel descended from one of these lines ? If so, the American branch have a right to its arms. That is the question on which we are now at work. The probable answer is, *Yes*. The family may rest assured that no rash surmises will be accepted ; but, if arms are published as belonging to the American branch, they will be authenticated. The compiler of the Genealogy, also, will insist upon firm ground.

These English investigations require means. The writer suggests that the Executive Committee be empowered to assume financial responsibility for English research in general ; research directed by the Secretary and compiler. In the course of such search, any arms to which the American branch may be entitled, would inevitably come to light. Should such not prove the case, let the family adopt a family device. This spirit is not snobbery, but a proper display of family love and appreciation. * *

We would say to every American family, to every descendant of the mighty men and noble women who here, in New England, founded a magnificent endowment of rugged strength and righteous fear in God,—to these we say .—

If in tracing the past, you find deeds and signs of mighty ones, whose spirits, *peradventure*, are even now observing if you are faithful to your inheritance, in the name of the strong God be thankful and treasure them!

Tell them to your children. Thank God for your heritage and live up to it !

The writer thanks those who have aided him in gathering these data, and acknowledges all sources. The data is given with due caution, and no surmises are stated as facts. By the next Reunion it is hoped things may be more fully established.

Mrs. Adna J. Fogg read a Paper on the same subject.—
She also exhibited a fac simile of the Fogg Coat of Arms, which gave great interest to the company :

Sir John Fogg:

Prepared and Read by Mrs. Adnah J Fogg.

Sir JOHN FOGGE, Privy Councillor, Treasurer, Comptroller of the Household of King Edward IV. He was a personal friend and a connection by marriage to the King. His first wife, Alice Haute, being first cousin to the Queen, Lady Elizabeth Woodville.

Sir John Fogge was Keeper of the Wardrobe to King Henry VI, in the last year of his reign ; and no doubt his change from the Red Rose of Lancaster to the White Rose of York, was due to his marriage connection with the Woodvilles.

He must have played a conspicuous part in the stirring events of that distracted time ; such as the banishment of Lord Warwick and the Duke of Clarence, the expulsion of Edward IV and the restoration of Henry VI.

His counsels, if not his personal services, doubtless assisted in the subsequent invasion of France, and the many curious negociations which ensued.

How he escaped the fate of Lords Riveo, Hasting, Grey, and others, seems surprising ; for no time was lost by Richard IV, on becoming King, in the attainder of Sir John, and in dispersing him of all his possessions.—
Perhaps he lay concealed or escaped abroad. Possibly he might have been amongst the two thousand followers of Henry, Earl of Richmond, (afterward Henry VII,) when he landed in England, or was one of those who played a

part in the Battle of Bosworth Field ; for the removal of
the attainder, and the restoration of his estate occurred in
the first year of the reign of Henry VII, who married
Elisabeth, daughter of Edward IV, and second cousin to
Sir John's wife.

The remaining six years of his life were spent in peace-
ful possession of his restored fortune ; and doubtless in
setting his house in order, preparing for his departure,
which occurred in 1499.

Sir John Fogge was more than once Sheriff of Kent
County. His benefactions to the town and church at
Ashford, were numerous and valuable   He restored or
rebuilt the bell tower ; enriched the church porch ; greatly
adorned the high altar, and bestowed many jewels ; ''all
which, (as an inscription observes,) was manifest to the
sight, and to be kept in remembrance by posterity, to the
praise of the Lord.''

In order more effectually to perpetuate the devotional
deeds of his life, he bequeathed to the town of Ashford, in
trust, lands and houses, for the maintenance of the church
and worship of God therein.

He was buried beneath a handsome altar tomb, between
the chancel and Fogge Chapel, which retained until 1644
the greater portion of its original ornaments, consisting
of brass effigies of himself and his two wives ; he being
attired in rich plate armor, and decorated with the Yorkist
collar of suns and roses, with the white lion of March
attached. His head rested on his helmet which is adorned
with mantling and crest. At his feet sits an Italian grey-
hound   On either hand lie his two wives, their mantles
fastened with roses ; at their feet crouches a dog. On one
of the three sides of the tomb, which was enriched by
panelling of Gothic arches, were three shields of Arms ;—
that to the right bearing Valoignes, impaling Fogge.
The shield had the arms of the first wife, Alice Haute ;
and propably the third contained those of the second
wife, Kuel.

On the front of the tomb, the center ornament was an
angel, supporting an inscription plate, within a circle of
rose sapling sticks firmly bound together, to represent the

stability of family unity.   These were all destroyed in 1644, excepting the helmet and crest.

A humorous vocal solo was rendered by Clarence E. Fogg, of Newburyport.

The Rev. John Blake Fogg, of Monmouth, Maine, continued the exercises with an Address. " Why should we Assist in Preparing a Genealogy." It was a blending of wit and eloquence ; and was a marked feature of the day's program.

A Poem, written by W. LeRoy Fogg, of Portsmouth, N. H., was read by Louis E. Fogg, of the same city ·

Verses :

Written by Walter LeRoy Fogg, and read by L. Everett Fogg

Of stern old stock is the clan of FOGG,
Of sinew sure, like a maple log ;
There's nothing brackish in the blood,—
It runs like a deep, clear river's flood.

Then what care we if sunbeams fail,
And the rain beats down on the sloping shale ?
Nor leaking skies nor sullen seas
Can dull this good day's pleasantries.

We meet in familywise once more,—
The slap of the surf on Hampton's shore
But echoes the happy songs we sing,
For light hearts form our offering.

Long matured is our family tree,
Far down the years runs our pedigree ;
A pedigree both long and strong,—
Then where is the weather can stop our song ?

Family pride has brought us here,—
Our escutcheon is bright and clear ;
All honor, then, to him who came
Across, and planted here our name !

All honor, again, to SAMUEL FOGG,
Who dared the waves like a bluff sea dog!
Unflinchingly faced the Ocean's frown
And found his haven in Hampton town!

Then, the seabird's wild, weird song,
Was undisturbed by the trolley gong ;
Cottagers had not come and made
Of Hampton Beach a long parade.

Now, the tourists throng this way ;
Autos whizz, musicians play ;
Hum and clatter fill the air,—
Modern life is everywhere.

Could Samuel Fogg today be here
And share with us this wholesome cheer,
Methinks we'd note a great surprise
Shine forth from out his honest eyes.

And then a smile would wreathe his mouth,
As he saw Foggs here from North and South,
From East and West, in proud array,—
And raising his hand to bless, he'd say :

" May all with the good old name of *Fogg*,
Show the stuff that's in a maple log;
Be it up hill, down, o'er dale or bog,
Go through this world at a steady jog !"

Next followed very interesting—

Five Minutes Talks ;

then one hundred and ninety-eight names were registered.
Seven Letters were read from interested cousins who
could not attend.

After various votes of thanks, the exercises closed with
the familiar melody,—

> Blest be the tie that binds our hearts in mutual love.

At the meeting the Rev. John B. Fogg, of Monmouth,
Maine, exhibited the watch and the saddle bags of his
grandfather, Rev. Caleb Fogg, who was born March 17,
1762, and died September 6, 1839.

The oldest attendant was Jeremiah R. Fogg, of Amesbury, Mass., born March 29. 1823.

Fogg Family. Third Reunion.

AUGUST 31, 1904. PORTLAND, MAINE.

With bright skies overhead, and faces reflecting the cheerfulness of the day, the Third Meeting of the Fogg Family Association was held in Harneou's Hall, Portland, Maine, August 31, 1904.

(G. R Fogg, Skowhegan, Me , Sec. pro. tem.)

The meeting was called to order, at eleven o'clock, by the President, the Rev. John Blake Fogg, of Monmouth, Maine. After the song of welcome, a prayer, touching and sincere in expression, was offered by him ; and then he proceeded to give the address of welcome :

Address of Welcome.

Rev. John Blake Fogg.

I am informed by the program of the Fogg Family Association that I am to give an address of welcome :— Now I am more than pleased to meet you in this hall, and look once more on your pleasant countenances.

It has come to be a real custom of State, to now have the Old-home Week, when those who have gone out from the old family home, town, and state, return to the old homestead, to meet again relatives and friends around the hearthstones, and look again on the fields and forest where they spent their childhood days, and spend a few days visiting the spots dear to us. With what pleasure we remember the old school house, with long wooden benches for seats ; and the many scholars who sat on them in our youthful days !

And I welcome you to-day, as we have gathered in this hall, as one great family. After years of wandering outside the old home circle, and located in many states and towns, we have gathered.here to pass a pleasant hour, and to get better acquainted with our great family ; and inquire somewhat into each others interest and welfare ; and come into sympathy with each other in legitimate interests, and truly be one great family of brothers and sisters.

May we make proper use of this hour, so that the memory of it in after years will give us pleasant recollections •

I welcome you to all the good things of this great country. You are here to properly enjoy them. Our fathers and mothers labored, toiled and suffered much that we should enjoy what we do today. The mighty forests have been laid low by the strong arm of the pioneer ; the log cabin has given place to the palatial mansion, and with the improved machinery, labor has been reduced to a minimum.

The productions of this country ought to satisfy the most fastidious both of body and mind. Think of the enormous crops of wheat and corn, annnally produced in this land of ours! almost enough to feed the population of the world. And in the Southern States, immense quantities of cotton are produced to supply the demands of our nnmerous cotton mills, which we find all over this land. From prairie states and mountain states of the West. come large quantities of wool to be manufactured into goods for mankind here and in other realms

Then each side of our land is washed by the waves of an ocean,—Atlantic and Pacific,—and these oceans are one vast store house of food to feed our large population And it costs nothing but the time and expense of catching and caring for the fish properly, to make the best of food for our millions

Now I have fed and clothed you, the body has been well cared for ; but we have done nothing for the *Mind*,— the most valuable part of of our being —

Now, what are the requirements of the mind, and what does it need for proper improvement? It needs to be educated in the best manner possible. Where can this be found? In most of the towns in this large country, an education can be procured, that will qualify anyone to do the business of the position which he may be called to fill, in any location in which he may reside If he desires a better or more thorough education than he can get in the country towns, he can find all grades of schools near by, up to old Harvard to graduate from

I welcome you to a land filled with all the modern improvements of this late age. We have in this country over two hundred thousand miles of railroad. It is like network, in all the States The trolley cars you find almost everywhere, running from city to city, and from village to village; a source of great convenience and comfort to every community, and helps much to expedite business And you find the telegraph and telephone office in almost every town of any importance in a business line all over this land,

Would time allow we could more minutely speak of the vast mineral wealth of this country. Gold, silver and coal are perhaps the most abundant ; and millions of men find employment working these extensive mines, located in many of the States of the Union.

I welcome you to a Country with the best Government in this world. Mankind are the best protected in all their interests and well-being of any land the sun shines upon.

I welcome you to a land of Religious Liberty! When the Pilgrim Fathers landed and offered a prayer to God, on Plymouth Rock, it almost seems as if God opened the portals of Heaven, and said to them :

I will give to you this Land, for a Paradise of Man's Freedom and Religious Liberty.

O call it Holy Ground,
  The spot where first they trod ;
They left unstained what there they found,—
  Freedom to Worship God !

We are on the stage, acting in the great Drama of Life. Let us act our part well and nobly. Do all that lies in your power to add to the happiness of your friends to-day Even though it be but little, neglect it not.

Do not wait until next month, or next week, or even until tomorrow, thinking you may be more able. They may not be here then. Though it be but a flower by the wayside, if it has beauty and fragrance, pluck it, and hand it to your fellow traveler; for if you wait to do great things for them, they may have fallen from your side and disappeared before you have done aught to gladden their souls. The day is short, but there is time for good and mighty works in it, and if we would be happy we must

gladden the present moments for another   There is a joy
and a work in each moment.   Seize it before it is too late.
Happy is the heart that at night can be conscious that the
day was well-spent ; and that we have made some one
happier,—and honored God !

—At the close of the Address of Welcome. Mrs Ella
Fogg Hasty, of Limerick, Maine, read the following
original Poem ;

Welcome of the Portland Pines.

Composed and Read by Mrs. Ella Fogg Hasty

The Portland Pines by the calling sea,
Messages bring to you and to me
Welcome, Welcome,—the Evergreens say,—
Tossed by the wind of this August day,
Hearts that are loyal, hearts that are true,
Listen! for we are akin to you.
When pulses electric pass through the air,
And the wind and the storm are everywhere,
Our branches question the threatening sky,—
Upward we reach,—and *wait the reply !*
Purple of morning, darkness of night,
Give us measures of rest and delight.
Through the summer's shine and winter's snow,
We use all our gifts and higher grow.
Kinship liveth not for *itself* alone,—
The soul that seeketh, shall find its own.
From a dismal land of fog and rain,
Where wind-gods strive by the raging main,—
From Norman conquests, from England's leas,
Our ancestors, from over the seas,
Have brought a heritage, true and tried.
—May it ever in our hearts abide !
Valor in war,—on the battlefield
With *Peradventure* upon the shield,
Just in all justice—love for the home—
Brave to face danger, whate'er may come.
Peradventure, we may sometime rise
To see our dreams materialize—
To learn that Art and Artist can

Idealize the world's rudest plan.
Kinship's an artist, its lines we trace
In every lineage of our race.
Today, the Foggs have assembled here
To greet their kindred and friends most dear;
To learn of the past—for the future plan—
And all of the good (?) Fogg family scan!
Great wealth have some, and character too,
The fortunes of others less plainly in view;
Philosophy, too, is much in our line,
Its achievements are our countersign.
The centuries live, yet the same race,
Akin in character and face,—
Youth with its hopes and age with its fears,—
Pass in and out of the changing years.
Shall our inheritance be in vain?
Shall we not strive, again and again,
Through trials, aye failure, to fulfill
The mandates of the Eternal Will?

  Dark Norway Pines, on their rugged height,
Companions of the storm and night,
Teach us to lift, when the clouds arise,
Our troubled hearts to the bending skies;
To seek that kinship, supreme and wise,
That answers our prayers in His replies.

  Pines near the Casco, sing low, sing low,
In minor chords, of the Long Ago,
Of dreams that fade, of hopes that die,
And loved ones lost as the years go by,
Possibilities, that lead us on
Till the *quest* is o'er, the life-work done!
Is kinship harmony, near and far?
It takes its chords from the Morning Star.
So messages come to you and me
From the Portland pines, by the calling sea,
As hand clasps hand we unitedly
Welcome, welcome the *Fogg Family*.

The Poem of Mrs. Hasty left a pleasant impression ;
and addresses followed by members of the Association.
George Orland Fogg, of Boston, spoke of the great family :

Our Family Record.

George Orland Fogg.

It is not an easy task to prepare an address for an
occasion like this, where of course much is expected,
while no hint has been given as to the line of thought
desired.

Oratory has but little place in the history of our family;
and the simple facts of its career, furnish but scant material for interesting discussion Even such history as is
available and pertinent, has been assigned to abler
speakers, and there is left for me such discoursive gener-
alities as may present themselves.

Our family can hardly boast of a conspicuous record :
We are an unostentatious, common-place people, with
about the general New England average of representatives
in the learned professions. No great single names over-
shadow us and irritate us with incentives to live up to
their standard. We can boast of no multi-millionaires or
trust magnates ; and we are not called on to blush for any
conspicuous criminals, who have been convicted. So far
as I know, none of us have been in jail, and none of us
are under indictment.

I am not certain but our family name is as well known,
the world over, not for its real members, but through the
imaginary adventures of that Yankee philosopher and
scientist, *Phineas Fogg*, who was created by that daring
romancer, Jules Verne.

Our record of mediocrity, however, will free us from the
familiar slur upon those who boast unduly of distinguished
ancestry,—that all that is good of us is like a potato crop,
under ground

It is something, however, to represent a family that has
grown up for a quarter of a millenium on the soil of New
England ; and under the pure influences of its domestic
life and civic surroundings. Even the harshness of creed
and the strictness of family government of the olden days,

are not to be condemned nor lamented ; for if we study them closely and trace their effect, we shall see how their limitatious gave strength, prudence, reverence and truth to later generations.

We have cause for thankfulness that the prepotency of these virtues is still so fully manifested ; for by this alone can the present and the coming generations hope to withstand and escape the influence of that moral laxity and indifference to the highest standards of life, that seem to be dominant factors in modern life. We hear much now of the sceptre of influence passing from New England; and that we who remain here must submit to the broad ideas and modern modes of thought and action, which control the newer sections of our great and growing country. But we need not fear. We know that in spite of the bluster and dogmatism which derides New England, the agencies and influences which have shaped and controlled the best and most potent thought of the whole country, had their birth and development amid our own surroundings, and by their own force have dominated and are still dominating the great States which lie towards the setting sun.

It should be our charge to keep this, the fountain of good morals and good government, pure. In no other way can we hope to influence and elevate the composite populations of those greater States, who, unfortunately for them and for the Country, are in need of teaching and example along the lines which have from the first controlled and blessed the people of New England.

As I look about me today, and see the representatives of this sturdy New England family, I am thinking of two words, which have within the year come into common use and constant thonght ; and curiously enough, both have come from a single source : the President of the United States :—*Strenuous* and *Race Suicide*.

Whatever our political faith, and however we intend to vote next November, we will all, I think, agree that a man who in a single year, thrusts upon the channels of popular thought, throughout a great nation, two ideas, is himself a man of power.

The word *strenuous*, has been in the Dictionary for
generations ; but it is safe to say that it has been used
oftener during the last twelve months than during the past
fifty years. You know what it signifies.—activity, vigor,
energy, eagerness, ardent, bold, zealous. Is it not worthy
of compliment and consideration that in these days of
indifference and laxity in almost all the walks of life,
except that of the money-getter, this word and all that it
embodies should receive as it were a new birth, and come
into our lives as a factor in bringing us life and action.

And the President's other word,—*race suicide!* He certainly forgot the good old New England habit of large
families, and the prolific qualities of modern immigrants,
if he meant to include in his reprehension the people at
large. It is probably true, and perhaps it is just as well,
that the frivolous devotees of modern fashion can be convicted under his indictment. Their habits and methods
certainly are not conducive to domestic life, and their
tastes and desires run in too selfish grooves to admit of
any care for posterity.

It is one of the late Henry Drummond's most earnest
contentions, that the earliest created germ of animal life
had in it, besides the instinct of self preservation, that of
care for others. The two primary life processes, he teaches
us, are nutrition and reproduction ; and on these the whole
fabric of human society is based. One is entirely self-
regarding, but the other has within its scope and potency,
all the joys and sacrifices of parenthood, domestic life and
philanthropy. In short it is the germ from which has
come all human advancement, and from which will come,
in God's good time, that which shall recreate and perfect
in the whole human race.

With this great, grand idea in mind, it is not strange
that the President should feel called upon to speak an
earnest word in behalf of harmony with God's purposes in
creation, and in condemnation of a social system which,
based entirely upon selfishness, is a clear violation of
nature's laws, which are God's laws, and so far as it is
promoted is a check on the onward and upward march of
humanity.

We of New England did not need either the inspiration

of his first word, nor the warning of his second. In fact the New England type is the *strenuous* one, as proved by her sons in the days of the old merchant and whaling marine, before steam was harnessed to do men's work, on the battlefield and in the subduing of the great wildernesses of the West, until they were fitted for the habitation of a less strenuous race. Good sized families are characteristic of our old New England stock ; and such families reared and taught to reverence and imitate the typical New England virtues are the salt of the earth , and by them, and such as they, is the nation to be strengthened and saved

With the opening of the new Century we enter upon an . era of inestimable opportunities. The forces of nature are coming more and more under human control. We live longer and do more in a month than our fathers did in a year. We are proud of the present and ambitious for the future. Let us take thought, however. lest we forget ! With all these privileges and opportunities come new duties and obligations. No man liveth to himself alone, —and this was never so true as today.

Personal Influence, rather than Preaching or Printing, is the Power that is to control the World for the coming centuries

We who have so grand a heritage of noble traditions, and the beneficent influence of heredity and environment, cannot afford to fail in making our own impress upon our time : not necessarily by great deeds,—for, are we not told, that the single mite of the poor widow. had weight above that of many greater sums in the Temple treasury.

One of the most interesting features of the Reunion, was the Paper of Dr. J. L. M. Willis, of Eliot, Maine :—

DANIEL FOGG, (second son of Samuel Fogg, the first,)
and his descendants.

Dr. Willis is a direct descendant, and resides on the ancient Fogg estate in Eliot. His paper, purely historical, gave a clear account of the early days of this branch of the early family :—   (*next page.*)

Daniel Fogg, of Eliot, Maine,

Second Son of Samuel the first, of Hampton, N H.

J. L. M WILLIS, M D

Before speaking of Daniel Fogg, you will pardon me if I ask you to glance with me a moment at some of his ancestors :

We live so much in the present, the passing hours are so thoroughly saturated with interests and duties, that a glance at the yesterdays seems an impossibility ; especially if that yesterday reaches back eight hundred years !

Our family name, *Fogg*, first appears on records shortly after the Norman Conquest , the Foggs were then among the dwellers of Lancashire, England. A little later we find them in Kent

The Kent county name, came into prominence three centuries later In the attractive Ashford town, not far from Wales, and fifty-four miles from London, there lived John Fogg, who had the prefix, *Sir;* and, better still. had the clear vision of the value of the parchments or books of his day ; and also a knowledge of them He made this mental perception to become perceptible fact, by founding a College

It was not a day when mental culture was easily attainable, or much sought,—in that year bordering on the date when Columbus discovered our America. But with Sir John, it was the new thought era of that far back yesterday Sir John evidently caught the gleam of a coming day , and immortalized his name by opening doors for the evolution of young men's brains

Three generations of Ashford Foggs, all titled *Sir*, can be traced , then the name ceases in the town of Ashford

We do not have proof that we of New England are of Ashford descent, yet we find the emigrant, Samuel Fogg, in Hampton, N. H , in 1638, and tradition says he came from Wales, the near neighbor of Ashford

Besides this proximity of early English homes, the descendants of our Hampton Samuel seem in close semblance to the Sir John and Sir Francis of Old England. Our New England has a Fogg-endowed Academy, (Berwick,) and a Fogg Public Library, also, a Fogg Art Museum at Harvard College. Besides, our own little town, Eliot, is to have a Fogg Memorial Library. The gifted chronologist, William Fogg V, has a name that will be perpetuated as long as people have any interest in records of families of old, old Kittery,—the corner stone of Maine history. (William Fogg V, was one of our earliest and most complete Maine genealogists and historians.) Such names as these seem like the evolved characters of the early English and Welsh names.

The Foggs, too, have another strong characteristic,—a love for pleasant places. When Samuel the first, (who was our own progenitor,) came to New England, in 1638, Hampton was his chosen home. It is one of the towns of natural beauty. We are not surprised that he established a home and gathered children and grandchildren about him in that attractive center

It is to this Samuel, our early grandfather, that we shall first glance; and then follow, if we can, the foot-steps of his son, who migrated from Hampton.

Samuel was evidently but a youth when he landed on our shores, in 1638. He did not marry for fourteen years. Then, on the tenth month, 12th day, 1652, he was united with Anne Shaw, of the town of Hampton. They were parents of four sons and one daughter. Two of the sons died in infancy.

Their youngest child was Daniel II, later of old Eliot town. When he was but a babe, his mother died. And Mary Page, (also of Hampton,) was the second wife, and the stepmother of the three surviving children of Samuel. She became the mother of two more sons and a daughter.

One singularity of this earliest Fogg family is their great age :—

Samuel, the firstborn, and his father's namesake, lived to be one hundred and seven years old;

Daniel, who was eventually engrafted into Eliot stock and life, reached ninety-five years ;

James, the second wife's son, died in his ninetieth year. It was evidently wholesome blood.

It is of Daniel II,—the youngest son of Samuel and Anne (Shaw,) that I am particularly to speak today:

He was left fatherless when he was twelve years old; and a great change came to his boy life. Soon after his father died, he was sent to Portsmouth, and learned the Blacksmith's trade; a trade of different scope then from now; for even a shingle nail was the fruit of the blacksmith's anvil.

When he became of age, he chose Scarboro as his home; and he found most congenial associates, for the Libbey's lived there,—a family of firmest character and solid worth, and eventually Hannah Libbey became his wife.

Substantial character and life, however, did not ensure permanency of comfort and home. It must have been a wretched existence in that day when people of a town had to huddle together in one house at night, and keep a loaded gun within grasp by day.

In 1690 came the dreaded attack, that caused Daniel II and Hannah his wife, and the two firstborn children, to flee to Portsmouth

As late as 1722, September 15 and 17, Military Officers and the Selectmen held a meeting to see what houses should be " Defencible in Kittery," by " Virtue of an Act of ye Government;" and one of these houses was Mr. John Rogers', near Green Acre, (Long Reach,) Eliot And all the families along the river, from Mr Rogers "to Daniel Fogg, Jun'r, Inclusively, Lodge therein."

Daniel Fogg had rather a lonesome new home in Portsmouth, when he fled thither, though one of exceeding beauty. There is a tradition that he was located oa a Portsmouth island, in the midst of the mile-wide Piscataqua. The broad world could not have given a more picturesque home. Five of his nine children were born in this family nest

But in 1699, a new plan was projected. The matter was discussed, and the decision was reached, that once more the Foggs and the Libbeys and others should live side by side. And they chose the lands in Eliot, that are yet held in the names of their descendants,—two hundred years of continuous ownership! It seemed, doubtless,

to both families, like beginning life anew. This new life
was on lands that for convenience, as well as beauty could
hardly be excelled.

The Scarboro house he gave in later days to his son,
John III ; and the father said he gave it to John, "In consideration of ye Parental Affection which I have towards
my well beloved Son."

We are interested to gather from records the description
of this Scarboro home and estate :

"Six Acres of Land, more or less, as it was granted to
me by ye Select Men of Scarborough, on ye 21st day of
Feb'ry, 1683, lying near the Meeting House ; thirty-six
Acres, more or less, lying at a Place called the Beaver
Damm, granted me by the select men of Scarborough,
aforesd, on ye fifth day of Feb'ry, 1684. One Island of
Marsh, in Scarborough afores'd, lying above Casco Bridge,
so called, containing about half an Acre, granted me by
ye Select men of Scarborough, on ye 4th day of May, 1685:
Twelve Acres of Marsh, lying above ye clay pits, so called,
adjoining to Thomas Larraby's Marsh, granted me by the
Proprietors of Scarborough, aforesd. And laid out and
bounded by the Lot layers, on ye 27th day of June, 1720 ;
the said grant bears date ye 22nd Day of the same June."

The purchased lands of Daniel II, in Eliot, were on
what we now term *The Old Road*, and at its very beginning, or entrance. It was an ancient Indian trail, and
probably the most ancient white man's path in Maine.
To the stranger of today, entering Eliot on an electric, if
he leaves the car at Fogg House. the present home of the
WILLIAM FOGG LIBRARY, he will step at once into the
Old Road, which runs directly through the Daniel Fogg
estate ; and a five minutes' walk will bring him to the
site of the Daniel Fogg home. The old house and hearthstone long since departed ; but the outline of the cellar is
discernable.

Let us open the gate, walk through the summer grass ;
we near the brook that runs into Fogg's Cove ; and here,
on the left is the cellar. The name of the Cove has been
changed. It has been Nutter's Cove ; and when Horace
Parker, the schoolmaster, married into the Fogg family,

it became Parker's Cove. But to this hour, if one calls
it Fogg Cove, it is understood.

Daniel Fogg had his eye on family conveniences ; for
there are several springs near by, and neither wife nor
child should thirst for "clear, bright, sparkling water,"
even if the winter cellar was supplied with the Puritan
cider barrels.

But, more beautiful than all, was the outstretch of the
Piscataqua, in full view of his western windows. The
winter winds might sweep up the broad stream,—nor
wind, nor storm could change the attraction of the wide
and wonderful view of river, a mile in width and never
frozen over   It was the same with the Libbey homestead,
—the father and mother of Hannah Fogg ; it doubtless
came to their Puritan minds, like a picture of the " River
of the Water of Life."

And the family enjoyed the domestic help the river
afforded ; for it was rich fishing and hunting ground.
The wild ducks came up the river in vast numbers; it
was a famous deer place ; (and roasted ducks and venison
are still most eatable luxuries) Fish were caught by
lines, nets and seines   The old-time seining would be a
novelty now   To this hour the memories or traditions of
the old fishing canoes have not faded. We can, in imagination, see them take the body of a massive tree, peel the
bark, and, when dry, hew and dig at the solid wood ; and
queer indeed, after the Indian fashion, set the center
aflame, that the fire might gnaw away at the center of the
log ; and when the great lengthy fragment of the pine was
made as hollow as a bucket, then it was smoothed and
seated ; and the *dug-out* was the fishing boat and the con-
veyance of travel.   They sailed from Long Reach to
Portsmouth, or to lower Kittery, up to Dover or Old
Quamphegan, in this old-time canoe

But the history of Daniel Fogg's Eliot land, must not
be omitted   It has a story, and blends some of the wisest
and the best of Eliot's earliest names ·

The Eliot home of Daniel dates from the 18th of December, 1699, the date of the deed   It is styled .

" A certain tract of Land, Scituate and Lying at a

certain place Commonly Called and Known by the name
· of Mr. Knowles his Purchase."

Knowles was the Dover minister, and became lonesome,
or weary, and went to the old England home ; and his
" Purchase" was returned to the control and possession of
Massachusetts

The next proprietor was Major Thomas Clark, "merchant of Boston." Major Clark died very soon after
possessing this land on the Long Reach, and the estate
fell to his co-heirs, who are called —

" Co-heirs,—Mehitable Warren, widow, and Elisha
Hutchinson, Esq., and Elisabeth, his wife, of Boston."

And of these "co-heirs" was it purchased by Daniel
Fogg, and four others, for "ye summ of three hund-
pounds, currant money."

In 1682, this stretch of territory was surveyed, and laid
out "by the allowance of Massachusetts," and recorded as
"240 rod in breadth, between Watts ffort and ffranks ffort,
running towards York five hundred and eighty rods
northeast and by East, and containing 870 acres in ye
whole, (reserving out of this sale Thirty Acres xx in ye
Possession of Joshua Downing "

These acres were "conveyed and confirmed" unto and
became the homes of Daniel Fogg and his friends,—the
names recorded in the following order .

Joseph Hammond, Esq., David Libbey, Matthew Libbey
Daniel Fogg, (ffogg,) Stephen Tobey.

The division of the Long Reach land of these five new
citizens of Eliot, or, as the deed calls it, the "Knolles
Purchase," occurred March 21, 1700, with their "mutual
agreement,"—no arguments, no dissents.

" Said Hammond is to have his part on ye North west
side of sd tract of land ;

and Daniel ffogg next to sd Hammond ;

and Matthew Libbey next to sd ffogg ;

and David Libbey and Stephen Tobey next to sd David
Libbey, being ye Lower most or Southeast side of sd tract
or parcel of Land xx ;

Joseph Hammond, Eighty and eight poles of sd Land
in breadth, and to run ye whole Length of sd tract ; xx

and ye other four men are to have thirty-eight poles
apiece, their lands with the exception of Hammonds,
butting upon ye Main river.''

Hammond had one-third part of the purchase of this
land between Watts and Franks Forts ; and he was prevented from reaching the river by the ownership of thirty
acres by Joshua Downing. The said Downing received
these acres, at the date of his marriage, from Dennis
Downing, his father. It was the home of Dennis as
early as 1652

Joseph Hammond also owned territory now familiarly
called Green Acre, on the Long Reach, and his possessions are still in the Hammond name. This Knowles
purchase was long known on record as '' The Bay Lands.''

On the beautiful Long Reach of the Piscataqua, was
the home of our first Eliot ancestor. The very lands over
which his descendants walk to-day, were once his own
footpaths   Here two of his sons built their homes :—

Joseph Fogg III, son of Daniel II, married Sarah Hill,
and built, on his father's lands, a house near that now
possessed by Joseph Kennard—opposite the William Fogg
house, now (1904) the Library

Daniel Fogg III, son of Daniel II, built the home now
possessed by myself ; and when he decided to move to
Scarboro, his brother James took possession of the home
he had erected on his father's farm

John IV, son of Daniel III, grandson of Daniel II, lived
next beneath the sheltering roof.   Then came the children
of John IV, names yet remembered by the aged ·—

There were John V, and his wife, Mary (Staples,) and
William V, of whom we have already spoken ; and of
whom we again repeat that he will be remembered and
his name spoken as long as people are interested to trace
Eliot and Kittery genealogies ; for his tireless intellect,
his love for the history, the names and localities, his
complete familiarity with long lines of pedigree, will keep
his printed records in constant use

William Fogg V, and his brother John V, lived upon
and owned the original and undiminished farm of Daniel II
of Eliot   John lived in his grandfather's house, (now

Dr. Willis's,) and William built himself a home which is the most historic of the later Eliot mansions.

But we must return again to the Daniel Fogg II, who was the first of the name to settle on the Long Reach; for there are pleasantly retold traditions of this early home of our name. We use the word *Pleasant.* Perhaps all the old-time memories could hardly respond to that expression for he lived in a day often clouded with uncertainty and fear.

Daniel II was evidently a man of fine physique and of strong personality. Aged people have told us traditions that he was six feet, one inch in height; with a face and voice that had immediate Influence. The tradition goes farther, and asserts that he was a noticeably handsome man. This strong personality brought him into the public duties of the town. His name appears in the lists of various public officers.

It has been the same, too, of others in succeeding generations.' It is rarely that we find a Town Meeting, that did not include in the official lists the name of Fogg. They have been of the peculiar mentality that naturally suggests them for public responsibilities; and, like Daniel II, have been sought for consultation and advice. And the review of two centuries reveals the fact that Daniel led forth a family line which has had peculiar recognition of the needful and the progressive in the passing years.

We find in the religious thought of his day that he was a leader. In 1721, June 22, he was one of seven men who united to organize, or as they termed it, to be "incorporated as a Church." The names in their written order were : John Rogers, Joseph Hammond, Samuel Hill, Nicholas Shapleigh, Stephen Tobey, Daniel Fogg, James Staples. Nearly or quite every home of these men was on or near the banks of the Piscataqua. We gather from the record the manner of this "incorporation ."—

The day was announced as a " Special Fast " The Rev. Nathaniel Rogers came across the ferry from Portsmouth ; Mr. Newmarch, the Kittery pastor, preached ; the Rev. William Shurtliff concluded with prayer, which was probably as long as the sermon.

This service was held in the little Meeting House, on
Long Reach, now a part of the homestead of William
Remick.   Then the three ministers went to the Rev. John
Rogers' house,—the Pastor-elect.   With them assembled
the seven men.   A confession of faith was read to them,
and when each had spoken an assent, the Rev. Nathaniel
Rogers, of Portsmouth prayed.   As he uttered the *Amen*,
the Church was declared—"Incorporated."

The females of the new Parish were received into
communion on the following Sabbaths.

But it was not always the quiet of Fast Day worship
There are traditions of fear in the Fogg family,—an ugly
and determined Indian attack on the Fogg homestead.
The Joseph Hammond house was the resort at night ; and
later, the John Rogers (farmer,) house.   It was appointed
by town authorities that the Libbeys, Foggs and Tobeys
should all shelter themselves in these Hammond and
Rogers houses ; and port holes were made under the eaves,
and even a palisade surrounded the Hammond shelter for
a season.

But one day in the broadest, brightest sunshine, the
Foggs discovered the dreadful and unmerciful enemy at
their very doors !   It was a moment of terror, but a moment that must be faced :   Madame Fogg at the instant
bolted the doors, or barred them, as the style and custom
then was.   She and her children asserted themselves,
giving commands, and pointing guns, as if a score were
within, ready to scatter shots and bullets at any moment

The Libbeys, close-at-hand neighbors, soon scented the
condition of things, and aided in a way that makes us
smile   They were devoting the hour to transforming
grease into old-fashioned *soft soap ,* and the Indians were
not over and above delighted to find themselves spattered
with boiling grease, direct from the kettle.   They concluded to depart without the desired "spoils of war."

This tradition of the Indian attack, and the effort to
become possessed of household desires, confirms itself by
Indian relics which we have found in the vicinity of the

early house,—the tomahawk, the arrows, the sinkers, have been now and again unearthed—traces of vigorous effort at some time. If these relics of savage warfare only had voices! but, silence is sometimes speech.

As the Libbey home adjoined the Daniel Fogg house, and as Hannah Libbey became Mrs. Daniel Fogg, we may tell another tradition, which has more of the smile than the terror :—

One of the Tobeys rode up to the Libbey house on horseback. Without dismounting, he rapped with his whip-handle on the front door. He was not heard by any of the family; so he reached to the bobbin latch, and, pulling the string, the old-time door swung open, and Tobey, with the dignity of a General, but with a suppressed laugh, rode through the old-time hall, and out of the rear door into the kitchen yard, where he discovered and surprised the indwellers, and delivered to them his errand.

That old, old Fogg Home! We wish a sketch of it had been saved But our early grandfathers and grandmothers never thought of pencilled memories, and it is doubtful if pencils were an acquaintance then. It would seem odd architecture today, with its great brick oven, out in the yard.

An aged relative who remembered the first Fogg home in Eliot, told us that it was a two story front, with upper windows close under the eaves; and in the rear was the steep roof, sliding down to the very door. Quaint as it would be to us if it still existed, it sheltered a worthy household, and the old hearthstone voices echo yet.

And when we think of its later children who bore the name of Fogg, and the veritable traits and disposition, bestowing rich legacies on academies, colleges and towns, which honor their names and magnify their gifts, we again turn back to that First Eliot Fogg House, and a wholesome respect floats over us; and we are glad that— The Old Road of Eliot, takes us to the summer fields and the cultivated lands of one who could add such strength of character and purpose to eight successive generations. We are glad of the retrospect ; glad of our name and its influence.

We are glad, too, that Daniel Fogg's *Grave* is yet pointed out, and that the old slate headstone bears his name : for even the knowledge of his grave makes him a character still real and his life an actuality.

The record of the previous meeting was read by G. R. Fogg, Skowhegan, Maine, Sec. pro. tem.

The report of Mrs. Adnah J. Fogg, of Boston, Treasurer, showed the Association out of debt.

Letters of regret were received from many sections of the country ; showing that the name and influence of our original Samuel Fogg, have reached all points of our fair America.

The Poem, " The Soliloquy of the Chair," was received with hearty cheerfulness It was written by Mrs. C. W. Fogg, aged seventy-seven years ; widow of John Sherburne Fogg, who was the grandson of Dr. Seth Fogg.

The chair is more than one hundred years old. It was the property of Dr. Seth Fogg, born at Epping, N. H., resided at Enfield, N. H. and later removed to Garland, Maine. It is now in possession of Donald Fogg, of Colton, California, grandson of John Sherburne Fogg

Soliloquy of the "Old Arm Chair."

By Mrs. C. W. Fogg, aged 77 years.

When I was young and strong and fair,
I was a Doctor's Office Chair ;
Full many years I served him well,
In Hampshire state and Maine as well.
And when his sands of life were run,
He gave me to his younger son ;
And when that son did win a bride,
They took me to their own fireside,
Where I, in state, sat many years
A witness to their hopes and fears ;
And when his work on earth was done,

He left me to his, younger son,—
California is now his home,
Where I with them from Maine did come.
One hundred years has made me old,
And soon my aged arms I'll fold ;
I know he'll treat me with much care
For I'm his own grandfather's Chair.
Just one more Fogg is now the heir,
To his own great grandfather's Chair.
Should he have sons and daughters fair,
I know they'll prize the Old Arm Chair!

Greetings to all Foggs everywhere,—
And farewell from the *Old Arm Chair.*

Rev. John B. Fogg, next called the attention of the
Association to three generations of sturdy Foggs,—showing clearly that, physically, the Foggs are not degenerat-
ing ; the youngest, nineteen years of age, weighing two
hundred and ten pounds !

The descendants of Seth Fogg sang *America ;* and
then came the—

Election of Officers:
Honorary President : John B. Fogg, Monmouth, Maine.
President : Elmer H. Fogg, Hartford, Conn.
Vice Pres.: Henry M. Fogg, Lowell, Mass.
        Gridley R. Fogg, Skowhegan, Maine.
        Samuel Fogg, Beverly, Mass.
Secretary and Treas. Mrs. Adnah J. Fogg, Boston.
Executive Committee :
        Frank A. Fogg, Laconia, N. H.
        George Osgood, Kensington, N. H.
        Edward H. Fogg, Manchester, N. H.
        Adnah J. Fogg, Boston, Mass.
        Henry M. Fogg, Lowell, Mass.
        George O. Fogg, Boston, Mass.
        Dr. A. S. Fogg, Norwood, Mass.
        Dr. F. S. Fogg, Roxbury, Mass.

At one o'clock, adjourned for dinner, at West End
Hotel.

The afternoon session was called to order at three o'clk. forty-five minutes :

Mrs. Adnah J. Fogg exhibited pictures of Lady Katharine Parr, who died in 1548. Queen consort of Henry 8.;

Of Queen Katharine's great grandfather, Sir Thomas Fogg, who died, 1512;

And of Katharine's great, great grandfather, Sir John Fogg, who died in 1490.

These pictures were accompanied by most interesting descriptions.

Mrs. Fogg also prepared and read the following brief Paper :

Katharine Parr, Fogg Descent.

Ortho Fogge came to Kent County, England, about 1272, and his grandson, Sir Francis Fogge, married Lady Joan de Valoynes, of Repton ; and their son, Sir Thomas Fogge, married Ann, Countess of Joyeaux, in Normandy. Their son, Sir Thomas Fogge, married Lady Joan, daughter of Sir Stephen de Valence. Their son, Sir Willian Fogg, married ———, daughter and heir of Septvaus of Ash. His son, Sir John Fogge, married first, Lady Alice Haute, daughter of Sir William and Joan Woodville, who was aunt to Elisabeth Woodville, wife of Edward IV. Sir John Fogge married 2nd, a Croil or Kriel. Their son, Sir Thomas Fogge, married Lady Elinor Brown. Their daughter, Lady Jane Fogge, married Sir Thomas Green. Their daughter, Lady Maud Green, married Sir Thomas Parr, and their daughter, Lady Katharine Parr, married

First, Lord Edward Burgh ;

Second, Lord (John Neville) Latimer ;

Third, Henry VIII, of England.

Fourth, Lord Thomas Seymour.

Letters,—written one hundred years ago,—by Major Jeremiah Fogg, of Kensington, N. H., were next exhibited. One of them was read; and expressed his views of the Louisiana purchase of that date.

A vote of thanks was extended to George E. Fogg, of Greene, Maine, for providing for the day's entertainment.

The oldest person present, was H. H. Fogg, of Bangor, Maine.

A suggestion was made by Rev. John B. Fogg, that a memorial service be held for those who should depart during the year.

A solo was rendered by A. M. Fogg, of Hebron, Maine, —received with hearty applause. Miss Winifred Robinson, of Hartford, played the accompaniment.

The meeting adjourned; and all felt that the "tie that binds," had become more enduring.

Fogg Family. Fourth Reunion.

Elmer Harris Fogg, Hartford, Conn., the President, in the chair.

Henry M. Fogg, Lowell, Mass. Secretary pro tem.

The Association sang the pleasantly familiar hymn :—
Blest be the tie that binds,
and it was followed by prayer, by Rev. Edward Quincy Osgood, of Brattleboro, Vermont.

The President's opening Address was very appropriate :

The "Hearty Welcome."
Elmer Harris Fogg.

Brothers, sisters, kinsmen, and every member of the two tribes of Samuel Fogg, I heartily welcome you to almost the very spot where our forefathers first set foot on American soil, two hundred and seventy-five years ago. I welcome you to the city of Boston,—the city made famous throughout the world, as being the home of many of the great men of America.

It is here that men and women have thought, and carrying their thoughts into action, have benefited every American citizen. Here is Fanuel Hall, the Cradle of Liberty, where so many have met and listened to the stirring words of patriotism, that filled breasts with zeal and courage. The old State House, too, named by John Adams *The Birth-place of Independence*, which so forcibly brings to our mind such names as Adams, Hancock, Otis, and others who sat in its council chambers, and guided not only the affairs of this commonwealth, but those of our nation. There are other places.—the old North Church, old South Church, and many others that I will not stop to mention, that are of great interest to all America loving people.

I welcome you to the City about which a noted English-

man was once asked : '' What is the most noted of all you
have seen in Boston ?'' His quick reply was :. *The Women.*
I cannot personally vouch for the truth of this ; but I am
told on reliable authority, that no city in America can
boast of having more women of great and noble characters
than Boston.

And not the least among them is our beloved sister,
Mrs. Adna J. Fogg, who has labored incessantly, searching and researching through all the history of Samuel and
Anne (Shaw) Fogg, and Samuel and Mary (Page) Fogg,
and their children and their children's children, even unto
the ninth and tenth generations. Surely Mrs. Fogg has
been a great benefactress to the whole Fogg Family
throughout America ; and we are here today to encourage
her in the work of the Genealogy of this great family, and
to assist her all we can.

I welcome you to this Hall, where so many of us have
gathered today to get better acquainted one with the
other, and to talk of the happenings of earlier days   As
we remember those of our forefathers who have dared to
face any emergency, and have been willing to live for
others, and even sacrifice their lives, if need be, in order
that we, and all who live within the borders of our beloved
country, might enjoy its many privileges, it seems to me
that every one of us ought to rejoice because of the great
inheritance.   There is not one of us but has inherited
much, not silver or gold, but something far better and
more valuable,—namely, life and liberty, liberty of conscience and spirit ; and the most beautiful country in the
world in which to exercise this liberty.

Think of the opportunities that lie before every one of
us. Opportunities such as no other people in the world
enjoy, When we look out upon the beautiful forests, with
all their verdure, and behold that which sheltered us, and
the fields that clothe and feed us, and though we travel
thousands of miles north, east, south or west, we see
nothing but that which ministers to the wants of man,—
we must in our inmost soul exclaim: ''This surely is a
great inheritance.''   I think we would be very ungrateful
indeed, if we did not express our appreciation of these

great blessings by doing something, as did our forefathers, to help and bless the world about us. This should be the aim and end of life of every one who bears the name of —Fogg.

I am not here to boast; I am here to say that every one of you have good blood in your veins; and if I read history correctly, there is no better blood than coursed through the veins of our ancestors from the time we find the Foggs in Denmark, even before English was spoken in England.

When William the Conqueror had the Dooms Day Book compiled in 1068, we find the Foggs extensive land owners, and this desire to live close to the very heart of nature, and own large tracts of land, seems to have been one of the characteristics of this family, as you will find by reading the Genealogy which our Secretary is compiling. All the way through the early history, we find them leading a rugged and hearty out-door life; just the requirements to to insure the best of stock.

Now, if we have developed qualities that make health, bone and muscle, should we not turn our attention more especially to that side of life which tends to develope the intellect? Not that I think the Fogg family more than others are lacking in this respect, but if we expect to keep pace with modern ideas, and be the leaders in the important tasks of life, we must train the mind, and search out and solve the intricate problems all about us. As one of our speakers said last year: "I like the *strenuousness* of our President." He touched the keynote which should be seriously considered in this advanced day and generation.

Just note for a few moments the advancement made in a few of the vocations of life; and let us, as a family, ask ourselves if we have contributed our share to the progress already made.

We will note the progress on the *Farm.* It is only a few years since the farmer in the springtime put what seed he had left into the ground, after selling off the best; and in the fall, gathered his harvest to find just the common ordinary yield; but now he saves the best for seed. and working on a scientific basis, produces even new varieties of the most delicious fruit and grain, and reaps abundant

harvests. He raised his herds of cattle and sheep from
inferior stock, but now only the best does he save for
breeding purposes; and many times sends thousands of
miles in order to secure the choicest animals.

I read recently of one in the West, who had, by his constant study of plant life, made a cactus to bear fruit without thorns; and other worthless plants and shrubs to yield
fruit and be things of beauty. He so arranged his work,
that the very elements of nature must of necessity assist
him. We had what we once considered a worthless and
dry desert, but today it has been made in many places to
blossom like the rose; and all because some one has
stopped to think and plan out this magnificent work.

For the sake of those who have not had the privilege of
attending our previous Reunions, I will give you an idea
of the noble blood as found in the Fogg Family during the
13th and 14th centuries ·

We are as English as England is herself; and Kent
County, England, is where the Foggs took a firm and help-
ing hand in making England what she is.

History tells us that King Henry VIII, was far from
being a good and able King; yet during the last four
years of his life, his wife, Catherine Parr,—who was grand
daughter of John Fogg, and great-great-grandaughter of
Sir William Fogg, son of Sir Thomas Fogg of Canterbury,
and so on down a long line of Foggs,—was able through
her diplomacy, not only to escape the fate of the other
wives, but prevented many of the bad moves for which
King Henry VIII was noted. I think our Secretary has
her picture, as well as that of Sir Thomas Fogg, and a
number of other Foggs, who so ably assisted in making
the laws of the 14th and 15th centuries

We are proud also of the record of him who dared to
leave his own country, and face the dangers and privations of the new country, and his children, Samuel Jr.,
and Daniel, by his first wife, and Seth, James and Mary by
his second, all of whom were sturdy and noble citizens of
New England. We find in looking up the records, that all
these and their children, assisted materially in guiding
the affairs of the early colonies.

There is one thing that we as a family should consider seriously, (this applies to the young more especially,) and that is, a thorough education is indispensible to one who wishes to make the most of himself. Let us not think for a moment that after we have passed through the High School and College, that our education is complete ; or that we are fully equipped to fill any position ; for it has only just begun. Let us continue to search for and acquire all the knowledge possible.

It should be our aim to excel in whatever vocation we may choose. There are too many young men today who are willing to make light of whatever work they are engaged in, thinking that at some future time, when a great opportunity presents itself, they will then show to the world that they can make a great name for themselves. I tell you such a one is deceiving himself, for it is only by doing our very best at all times, and in every day duties which present themselves, that we become proficient and capable of taking charge of great enterprises and carrying them through to a successful completion.

What the world needs today is men and women with a large degree of stick-to-ativeness, combined with honesty and integrity. Thus equipped, the duties of today will be well-done, and the responsibilities of tomorrow well met, and the development of our characters will go steadily on, until the time when, with characters well ronnded out, we are willing to turn over to younger hands the duties of the hour, and commit to our Heavenly Father the threads of life we have tried to weave into a perfect whole.

The address of the President was immediately followed by a Solo,—Miss Marita Libbey Stephens, of Boston ; it was received with hearty applause.

Next came a paper of valuable family biography ; valuable as a chapter of the Town History as well. It was read by the Rev. Edmund Quincy Osgood, of Brattleboro. Vermont. It revived the memories of the Rev Jeremiah Fogg, who was born at the old Hampton homestead, 1712.

The paper was made more interesting when it was known that Mr. Osgood was the great-great-grandson of

the Rev. Jeremiah.   And a long-ago relic was exhibited :
a punch bowl, that figured at a Harvard Commencement,
and later, as a christening bowl, in Jeremiah's pulpit and
parish labors .

Rev. Jeremiah Fogg.
THE KENSINGTON MINISTER.

Prepared and Read by Rev Edmund Quincy Osgood.

The subject of this sketch.—Rev JEREMIAH FOGG,—
my great-great grandfather, was born in the town of
Hampton, New Hampshire, May 24, 1712.   He, himself,
was the son of Seth Fogg, who was born in Hampton,
Nov 28, 1666 ; and the grandson of our common emigrant
ancestor, Samuel Fogg, who came to this country before
the middle of the seventeenth century, (possibly in the
Arabella 1630,) settled in Hampton, and died there in
the year 1672.

According to the records, Seth received from his father
by will, the sum only of six pounds, to be paid him by his
oldest brother, out of the estate, all the real property
having been left to this eldest son, in harmony with the
custom then prevalent in England.   It is probable, however, that a certain portion of land was assigned him, since
he and his family evidently lived upon it in after life —
Then, too, the wife of Seth Fogg, Sarah Shaw, was the
grandaughter of Roger Shaw, one of the large landholders
of Hampton, and may easily have inherited a few broad
acres in her own right

Though not opulent in worldly goods, this worthy
couple were blessed with children ; no less than eleven or
twelve appearing one after another in their home ;—
Jeremiah having the honor of ranking the seventh among
the sons

No memorial is handed down to us of the inner workings and experiences of this large family   No doubt it
was a typical household of an early New England settlement, checkered by the sunshine and the shadows of the
period.

The boy, Jeremiah, must have shown some capacity as
a scholar, for he was prepared for Harvard College by the

time he was fourteen years of age,—his tutor having been
in all probability, the Rev Nathaniel Gooking, the minister of the Hampton Church,   He entered Harvard in 1726,
graduating in the Class of 1730.

Benjamin Wadsworth was the President of the College
during the boy's four years residence at Cambridge.
Among the Fellows, forming the Corporation of the College, at that time, were Edward Wigglesworth, Joseph
Sewall, Nathan Pierce, all personages destined to hold
positions of importance in the Massachusetts Colony.

The Class of 1730, numbered thirty-six in all. In com-
pliance with the custom then kept up at Harvard, the
graduates names do not appear in alphabetical order, but
according to the supposed rank or station in life, of each.
Thus Peter Oliver leads the Class, who, at a later date,
received the degree of Doctor of Civil Laws, from Oxford
University, and held the position of Chief Justice of the
Superior Court of the Province of Massachusetts. The
name of Jeremiah Fogg, is the thirtieth on his Class-roll,
with letters following it to signify that the degree of
Master of Arts was conferred in due course

The Harvard College of that day, was not the Harvard
College of this.   Nevertheless Commencement was observed with ceremony and feasting then as now, graced
withal by the presence of high dignitaries of Church and
State. As a token of this far off event in the life of my
ancestor, there has come down in the family from generation to generation, and is present with us today, a small
punch bowl, used by the lad and his friends, when bidding
farewell to their Alma Mater   Though not as handsome
(from an artistic point of view,) as the bowl used by his
son William at his graduation in 1774, (and which is still
preserved,) yet it appeals strongly to our interest, forming
as it does a single link in that chain that binds us to those
earlier colonial times

Fully 150 years after this bowl, with its quaint rim, had
been filled with Commencement punch, it held the sacred
waters of baptism, when my Uncle, (the Rev. George
Osgood of Kensington,) used it for a christening service,
in which figured as principals some Gypsy children, be-

longing to a summer encampment near the old Parsonage.

The six or seven years following his graduation, were evidently spent by Jeremiah at the Hampton home, where he was doubtless of service on the farm, and very possibly may have presided over the destinies of a District School, or, in some other way promoted the cause of education in the community.   His choice of a profession, however, necessitated the acquirement of a special kind of knowledge on his part ; so for a portion of this period, he studied Theology with the Rev. Joseph Whipple, of Hampton Falls, obtaining at the same time, some insight into the practical duties of a country minister.

Hampton Falls had been set off from Hampton, as early as 1712, and was called the West Parish. But as time went on, many people living in the outskirts of this Parish found it inconvenient to travel the four or five miles necessary to attend divine service, especially when the snow lay deep on the ground   Therefore the minister, Mr. Whipple, in connection with his society, was [in the year 1734.] authorized to employ some one to preach to these isolated members of his flock, four months during the winter ; thus forming what was then termed the Winter Parish.

In the following year a similar arrangement was made ; it being proposed, in the Hampton Falls parish meeting, to excuse the people in the upper part of the parish from the ministerial tax, in order that they might employ a minister themselves.

This Winter Parish, originally a part of Hampton, and after 1712 belonging to Hampton Falls, was incorporated in the summer of 1737, as a distinct township, receiving the name of *Kensington.* In October of the same year, fifty-seven persons, viz , twenty-two men and thirty-five women,, were dismissed from the Church in Hampton Falls, in order to form a new and separate religious society in Kensington. I will quote a paragraph or two from the records of this important meeting :

October 6, 1737 —Christ the great head of the Church, in his good providence, hath marvellously increased the number of the Christian Churches in this land, aud the same divine grace which hath built up others, hath planted a Church in this place.

" The several members of which the Church consisted, having sought and obtained regular dismission from the respective churches to which they belonged, requested the assistance of some neighboring ministers, to join with them in keeping a day of fasting and prayer."

Accordingly, " The Rev'd Ward Cotton of Hampton began with prayer. The Rev'd John Odlin, of Exeter, preached from Isaiah lvi : 6, *And taketh hold of my Covenant.* The Rev'd Joseph Whipple, of Hampton Falls, propounded to those there to be organized, a Church Covenant,"— whose tenets were in harmony with the belief of the Congregational Churches of the times.

But before this strictly ecclesiastical meeting took place, —that is to say, on the 17th day of June previous,—a legal meeting of the freeholders of the Kensington Parish had been called to make choice of a permanent minister. Nor is it strange that they voted to ask Mr. *Jeremiah Fogg* to fill this position; he was undoubtedly well known to them all, being a member of an important family residing in the parent town of Hampton. Furthermore it is very possible that he had frequently accompanied his instructor and spiritual advisor, the Rev'd Mr. Whipple, in his various services for these outlying communicants in his charge.

The following votes, passed at this meeting, are of interest in this connection :—

Voted, that Mr. Fogg shall preach for us, until March, for forty shillings a day.

Voted, that Mr. Fogg shall have one hundred and twenty pounds the first year, and to add five pounds a year for eight years.

—At an adjourned meeting, July 11 :

Voted, to build Mr. Fogg a convenient house and barn, and dig him a well and stone it, and find him land to keep two cows and a horse summer and winter.

This arrangement was afterward changed ; and the Parish gave Mr. Fogg $1000 in money, with which he bought land and built his house.

Voted, that there be a consideration in the agreement about the badness of money.

Voted, to find Mr Fogg his wood as long as he shall be our minister.

At a meeting held October 4, it was—

Voted, that the fourth Wednesday in November, be the day for to Ordain Mr. Fogg.

Thus on the 23d day of November, in the year of our Lord 1737, began the ministry of Jeremiah Fogg in Kensington, which was destined to extend over fifty-two years, covering practically the remainder of his long life.

The sermon at the ordination was preached by Rev. Joseph Whipple of Hampton Falls, and the churches of the neighboring countryside were represented by pastors and delegates

From all that I can learn with regard to this life-ministry of my ancestor, it was pleasant and profitable both to pastor and people. The shadow hovering over the closing years of his faithful service, had its source in a frank difference of opinion respecting certain beliefs considered as essential to the well-being of the Christian Church, and not to any radical change, whether of character or ethical standards, such as (it is sad to say,) is sometimes the case

The house built by the young minister was finished probably in 1739; the well dug; and a barn erected a little in the rear of the house for his cattle. About thirty acres of land adjoined the homestead, and assisted in his maintenance

The house is situated on a slight eminence, with a pleasant view of cultivated fields lying before it, and a back-ground of orchard and pasture and feathery pines

It is pleasing to remember that this simple frame house, with its four square rooms in front, stands today very much as when it was raised by Mr. Fogg's parishoners 167 years ago   The ell now attached to it belongs to a later period, and some minor changes have been introduced from time to time. But it remains substantially the same.

The well, dug and stoned so many years since, still serves the purposes of the household ;—its mouth, open to the hot breaths of summer and the snows of winter, having seen myriads of buckets of cool, sparkling water drawn up by succeeding generations of the same family.

The barn originally built, was burned down about the time of Mr. Fogg's death ; but one constructed soon after, still remains, gray and weather-beaten, it is true, yet fit for many years more of honorable service.

Mr. Fogg had not labored for any lengthy period in this Kensington Parish, when his marriage took place, and a bride was ready to grace the newly-built parsonage.— On the 13th day of July, 1739, he took as his wife the only daughter of Rev. Joseph Parsons, the minister of Rocky Hill church, in the neighboring town of Salisbury, Mass

The charming tradition is handed down to us, that Parson Fogg rode to his new home over the Kensington hills, and through the pine forests, with his bride Eliz-abeth, seated on the pillion behind him It is also related that one of his deacons, who had attended the wedding at Rocky Hill, carried to the Parsonage in the same fashion, a colored girl, Phyllis by name, one of the domestics in the Salisbury household. but was now to wait upon her young mistress in the cozy manse that had been made ready for her.

In March, 1740, a few months after this marriage was solemnized, occurred the death of the bride's father,— Rev. Joseph Parsons, whose widow came to live in the Fogg Parsonage. She brought with her a colored man, already quite advanced in years, called Primus. Accord-to colonial law, both this man and the girl Phyllis ranked nominally as slaves. Primus, indeed, was the son of an African Chief But, in point of fact, they were devoted servants to the family, attached to every member of it by ties of affection, regard and mutual service. Sometime before the Revolutionary War, Primus helped his master set out two elm trees, at a short distance from the house. One of these died about 1850, but the other is still stand-ing, though showing many signs of decay.

The married life of Jeremiah Fogg and his wife Eliz-abeth, extended over a period of forty years ; or until the death of Mrs. Fogg, in 1779 Nine children were born to them, of whom eight lived to grow up. The first three were girls, named respectively Elisabeth, Sarah and Mary. Elisabeth in due time became the wife of William Parkhurst, who graduated at Harvard in 1751 ; and Sarah, married Ebenezer Potter ; Mary, or Aunt Mollie, (as she was affectionately designated,) was the spinster of the family, and lived on in the parsonage until her death in 1823. My father, Joseph Osgood, whose birth year was 1815, always retained a vivid recollection of this Aunt Mollie, and delighted his children with talks about her.

The fourth child, a son, died in infancy ; but the five sons concluding the list, all lived to take an active part in the stirring scenes that marked the latter half of the 18th century in our country. Of these five sons, four served in the Revolutionary Army.

The oldest of the five, Jeremiah, of the Harvard Class of 1768, received the title of Major, for distingnished military service ; and the noteworthy events of his career will be set before you at length in a separate paper.

The second of these five sons, Joseph, (my great-grandfather,) was commissioned Quartermaster of Col. Enoch Poor's Regiment, June 5, 1775 ; and went into quarters at Winter Hill, under Gen. Sullivan. At a later date he served with a Battalion of troops, raised to defend the States of New England. The tradition also runs in the family that he went to France, on board of a privateer, bringing back with him as a memento of his trip, a pair of wooden shoes, or sabots, to his favorite sister Mollie.

At the close of the war, in 1781, Joseph Fogg married Mary Sherburne, and they went to house-keeping in part of the homestead. In the course of two years his wife died, leaving an infant daughter, Elizabeth. Upon the second marriage of her father, and his removal from town, this little girl was practically adopted by Aunt Mollie, and until her death in 1869, she spent the larger part of her time in the Fogg parsonage, which eventually became her exclusive property. In 1811, she married Dr. Joseph Otis Osgood, of Andover, Mass. Four children of this marriage lived to maturity, viz., Elizabeth, Joseph, George and William. My father, Joseph Osgood, was her oldest son, who for fifty-six years was the minister of the First Parish in Cohasset, Mass., and died Aug 2, 1898, leaving five daughters and four sons to perpetuate the traditions of the family. His wife was Ellen Devereux Sewall, who passed away in 1892. The parsonage is now owned and occupied by my brother, George Osgood.

William, the third of those five sons of Jeremiah and Elisabeth Fogg, was born in 1755; graduated at Harvard in 1774 ; served as a soldier in the Revolution, and, later, taught in Fredericksburg, Va., and other places, dying unmarried in 1807.

The fourth son, Daniel, was born in 1759; he studied medicine. He acted as surgeon's mate towards the close of the Revolution, and finally settled as a physician in Braintree, Mass , where he died in 1830

The youngest son, John, born 1764, also became a physician, practicing for several years in North Hampton, where he died in 1816.

I have purposely made a brief mention of these children of Jeremiah and Elisabeth Fogg in this place, rather than at the end of my paper, in order that the life of the Kensington minister might be the central object of our interest to the very close of this rather incomplete biographical sketch. The care and bringing up of these eight girls and boys in the "nurture and admonition of the Lord," must have occupied much of the good minister's time, as well as that of his wife ; and drawn largely upon his strength. Nevertheless, there were numberless tasks in connection with his parish and farm, and his position as an important citizen of the little community, that demanded constant attention.

The first Meeting-house in which Mr. Fogg conducted services, was built on the west side of the brook, near the residence of Charles E Tuck, but later was taken down and moved to a spot nearer the centre of the town. The land for the old Meeting-house and graveyard adjoining, was given by Elihu Chase, but as the parish failed to reserve for him a pew, he left the society and joined the Friends. This structure stood until 1771, when it was torn down and another put in its stead. The last Sunday in the Meeting-house, May 12, 1771, Mr. Fogg preached from a verse in the 132d Psalm . *We wept when we remembered Zion.*

At the present day a more modern house stands in the place of the old, built, however, as far back as 1846 ; but the graveyard remains the same, shaded by pine trees, and marked by the old-time tablets of slate.

The records tell us that during Mr Fogg's ministry of more than half a century he baptized 1235 persons, young and old , the largest number in any single year being 39. During this time he solemnized 402 marriages.   How many communicants were received into the church, and the number of funeral services the worthy pastor performed, cannot now be ascertained with accuracy, since that portion of the records is lost

Every Sunday, probably, he preached twice to his Kensington flock, excepting when an exchange of pulpits with some neighboring minister in Exeter, or Hampton, or Salisbury, called him away.   These sermons, too, written in the finest of hands on tiny sheets of paper, (as was the custom of the day,) no doubt reflected at intervals the disturbed state of his country, and the fluctuations of the war of the Revolution, as it rose and ebbed.

Then, in his relation of Pastor, how many calls must he have made upon the families in his parish, from year to year ! What consolation must he have brought into houses of mourning !   What sound advice must he have given in cases demanding cool judgment and strict impartiality !

So far as I know, there is no portrait extant of Mr. Fogg ; but a silhouette, still to be seen, gives an idea of the outline of his face and of his bag wig.   He was evidently rather a stout man, with a short neck and broad shoulders.

He was renowned for his wit and humor, and liked to have people call at his house with whom he might converse about the chances of good crops, the political events of the day, or some theological question.

In a letter written late in life by John Adams to his classmate, David Sewall, telling of a journey he made about 1751, into New Hampshire, he says :—

" I recollect nothing worth recording in my tour, except that we called at Parson Foggs, in Kensington, where we had much conversation respecting Mr. Wibird, afterwards ,my minister, then much celebrated for the eloquence of his style."

It is probable that Mr. Adams stopped at Kensington, partly to see Madam Parsons, who was formerly an Elizabeth Thompson, of Braintree, Mass.

No doubt Parson Fogg was on excellent terms with all his neighbors and fellow-townspeople ; was interested in their plans and occupations , and was ready at any time to be of service to them when needed. Many of his own kindred lived only a few miles away in Hampton, whom he must have seen now and then, in order to exchange bits of family news ; while in Kensington, itself, his cousin James had a home within a reasonable distance of the parsonage. At that period more than at present, families were brought more closely together, and felt more deeply the ties of kinship, and the claims of a common descent.

As a scholar and preacher, Mr. Fogg, I have reason to believe, held a respectable place among the members of his profession. He was certainly an independent thinker, and possessed the courage of his convictions This is manifested very plainly throughout the closing years of his fruitful ministry, when his theological views began to be criticised.

" The Rev Jeremiah Fogg," says Bradford, "was ranked with the Armenians,—with the Rev Drs. Samuel Webster of Salisbury, Thomas Barnard of Salem, and William Symmes of Andover. * * These clergymen. and many others, gradually departed from the Calvinistic system, and forbore to urge or to profess its peculiar tenets * * They did not insist as a preliminary to the ordination of a young man to the Christian Ministry, his professing a belief in the Trinity, or the five points of Calvinism."

This quotation will show that Mr. Fogg was alive to the more liberal spirit, that in the latter decades of the eighteenth century, was beginning to be felt in the Christian Church. Indeed, he has sometimes been termed the

first Unitarian minister in New Hampshire. Consequently
it is not to be wondered at, that those of his people who
were most devoted to the type of theology handed down
by their fathers, resented this apparent defection, on the
part of their minister, and determined to call him to strict
account. Therefore, in January, 1789, and again in July,
of the same year, a Council was summoned to listen to
and to take action upon whatever charges might be
brought against him, with respect to the laxity of his
belief.

From a letter, which Mr Fogg wrote to the first Council,
I will give the following extract :—

" Reason, that divine mark of distinction in human
nature, was given us by the same Being who gave us the
Scriptures. And I have ever made it my practice to exercise it, in reconciling the more difficult passages in the
Sacred writings ; and, wherever I find gentlemen of education and ability, I find an inclination, as well as a duty,
to converse freely on subjects of controversy, that all may
be the better established in the religion of Jesus "

Mr. Fogg did not appear in person before these councils, but was represented by members of his parish, who
took the same reasonable view of these church doctrines
that he himself advanced.

But the outcome of the whole matter was, that Mr. Fogg
was obliged to give up his official connection with the
parish, to whose wants he had ministered so long, and, so
far as his material affairs were concerned, to be content
with a small pension and a certain amount of firewood,
annually, for the remainder of his life. It was not a
lengthy privation, however ; one that had hardly an
opportunity to be realized. For on Dec. 1, 1789, he died,
—ten years after his wife, Elisabeth , regarded with honor
and affection by the entire community,—not even excepting
those whose theological beliefs differed from his own.

He lies in the old Kensington churchyard, beside his
wife, and near the grave of Madam Parsons—two persons
who were perhaps the closest to him during the happiest
and most inspiring portion of his useful life. The inscrip-

tion on the stone that marks his resting place reads as follows :

" In Memory of the Rev. Jeremiah Fogg, A. M. who died Dec. 1, 1789, in the 78th year of his age, and the 52d of his ministry :

" Mark the perfect man, and behold the upright ; for the end of that man is peace."

A simple, yet well-spent life, is thus brought a little more vividly before us ; one that "fought the good fight;" that "kept the faith," as he understood it; that tried faithfully to do the Father's will.

" The Pastor more than fifty years,
    His people watched with care and love,
  And blessed them in their joys and fears
    With hopes of happier homes above."

George O. Fogg exhibited from the President's desk, a flint lock pistol, carried by his grandfather Fogg in the Revolution.

The talent of the Fogg Family was next revealed in an Ode, written for the occasion and read by the author :— Rev. Charles Grant Fogg, Staffordville, Ct.

Ode.

REV. CHARLES GRANT FOGG.

The singing of the pines upon the mountain slopes,
Where thunder-battled crags enthrone the eagles. Where
Before the northern blast, the swirl of driving snow
Sweeps o'er the wild fierce sea. The boom of raging surf
That leaps in crashing tempest on an iron shore.
The misty forests of the northern lowland drear.
The far, far vision of the heaving, flashing wave
That gleams in whitened sun, or leaps in frothy spume.
Such was thy joy, O Daneland ! Such thy rugged strength!
The stern but tender mother of a noble race,
Whose father was the mighty ocean ; in thine arms
Was reared the strength of mighty nations yet to be.
Grand motherland ! The home of nature's ruling race !

Thy giant fair-haired sons, whose piercing hazel eyes
Saw distant vineland beckoning o'er the western main,
Were kings of men, the restless eagles of the sea.
Thy tall, fair women were Queen mothers of a race,
The limit of whose realm should be the ocean's bounds.
Thou art the land of strength, of action, and of power.

Grand is the Northland! birthplace of the Viking's brood,
Who swept the Grecian seas, and hailed far Hecla's star.
But dearer are the wooded plains of England fair,
The land of hawthorn bloom, of moor and fen and glade
The land of the Great Charter, right of freeborn men
Who, knight and footman, side by side at Crecy's lane
Proclaimed that manhood is the nation's test of men.
Whose two great Queens, thro' many a year of prospering
        sway,
Elisabeth the mighty, Victoria the Wise,
In dignity and grace uplifted woman's throne.
Thou art the newer Daneland, where the common race
Of Goth, as Norman, Daneman, Saxon, tempered with
The fire of Briton, took the best of each;
And lo! a mighty race, whose mission to go forth
And bear the white man's burden, lifting up the world
From ignorance, injustice, prejudice and sloth
Thine is the land of Law! The Northman's active power
Transformed to justice, yet again to the great law
Or service due from man to every fellowman.

These were the homes of freedom, these our motherlands.
The wild free vigor of the Northland and the sea,
Tempered with gracious sweetness of the inland clime.
Dear is the memory of the rolling fields of Kent;
Precious the treasured centuries that cluster round
The walls of dear old Ashford. But more dear by far
The voice of freedom for God's worship and man's rights.
And when oppression's mist hung heavy on the land,
The northern river beckoned to the northern sea;
The sands of Gravesend and the cliffs of Dover's shore
Called with the voice that never Northmen heard in vain.
And far across the western waters a new home,
A brighter Daneland, a New England rose in view.

A city fair, a newer Vineland, where the huts
Of ancient Norumbega sheltered Eric's son,
And once again the Viking claims his Western home.

America, the land of freedom and of power !
Thou hast thy Canterburys, to thy children dear,
And sacred as the fane of thy ancestral home !
Dear the inspiring glories of St. Botolph's town,
Where freedom rose, triumphant, from restraining bars
Imposed by unwise counsel to an erring king,
Whose blind advisers drove the child from father's house,
Forgetful of the love of liberty that fires
The soul of every child of sires of Runnymede.
Hallowed the graves on Burial Hill by Plymouth's strand,
Where Mayflower's dauntless pilgrims, o'er a wintry sea,
Lay down to sleep, but rose to live forevermore,
And guide the centuries to the brotherhood of man
Proud Salem sits enthroned beside the northern sea,
Fair mother of a line of mighty sea-kings   Far
Into unchartered seas their rushing keels have cleft,
And made the Eastern lands a province of the West.

And thou, fair HAMPTON, home of our brave Sire who came
In flush of youth, and proved the weight of manhood's worth !
To thee our hearts return.   There the ancestral home
Still stands, with open doors, and bids us ever welcome.
We know no home so blessed with tender memories.
There are no fields so fair as thy proud acres green.
There is no sea so blue, no wave that calls so sweet,
As sea that flashes back the smile of summer sun,
And answers to the whisper of caressing breeze
That lulls the flowers to sleep on Hampton's lovely strand !
And thou, our noble sire ! thou mighty English Dane !
Strong was thine heart, thine arm of power, thy vision far !
Rich thine inheritance of noble sires, yeoman !
In newer lands thou left the ancient name renewed,
Where every worthy man is peer in manhood's realm !
Where every true-souled woman is a reigning queen !

Our part to hold the honor of the ancient name,
And in the spirit of our watchword overcome.
Almost three hundred years have passed since our brave
      sire
Came from his Kentish home to Hampton's sunny shore.

Stout of heart and arm, to ancient watchword true,
And we, his later children, and of those strong souls—
The mothers of the generations yet to come.
What do we today to show our watchword's power?
The age of chivalry is not yet past.   The joy
Of strife and overcoming is the same wild joy
That leaped in Northmen's veins. That strove at Seniac's
      field,
That fought with stout old Drake ; with Winthrop
      crossed the main ;
The fierce sweet joy of right, triumphant over wrong.
For still, today, oppression threatens as of old ;
Great nations sit in darkness, and wait the rising dawn.
And still the race that crushed the iron power of Rome,
That swept the Western seas, and in this Western land
Founded the newer empire of equal rights to all—
We are they whom God has chosen to go forth,
With Liberty and Justice, and the Golden Rule,
The measure of our statecraft and our love for man.
And peradventure if our lives are pure and strong,
If on our shield of gold is honor's record true,
We know that we are one of many families,
All joined in blood, in heart, and in the consciousness
That peradventure those strong souls who overcame
Still lead us on, and wait to give the victor's crown.

    At this hour of the meeting, Henry M. Fogg, of Lowell
Mass., Secretary pro tem, read the record of the last
meeting ;—

    Mrs. Adna J. Fogg, the Secretary and Treasurer, made
a statement of the finances, and read greetings that came
by mail from all sections of the country.

    These papers of interest were followed by a solo, by—

Miss Mary E. Fogg, of Gorham, N. H. ; the accompaniment played by Marion E. Shedd. The applause was unanimous.

At this point came a social hour, devoted to "becoming acquainted ;" and to the friendly words and voices of the great family. And when it was passsed,—

Gladys Perkins Fogg, entertained by songs ; and she was followed by Miss M. L. Stevens.

Several Papers were read at this hour ; the first by Mrs. Charles A. Hillard, Lynn, Mass.

Jeremiah Fogg,

Of the Order of the Cincinnati, and his Descendants.

By Mrs. C. A. Hillard, Lynn, Mass.

Jeremiah Fogg, eldest son of the Rev. Jeremiah and Elizabeth (Parsons) Fogg, was born in Kensington, N. H in 1749 , being the fourth in line from Samuel the first. His father, " Parson Fogg," as he was familiarly called, was the son of Seth, who was the son of Samuel by the second wife, Mary Page.

He was graduated from Harvard College in 1768, after which he spent several years teaching in Newburyport, Mass , where he commenced the study of Law, being considered one of the ablest jurists of the day.

At the beginning of the War, he entered Col. Poor's regiment ; and continued in the service until the close of the Revolution. It would be needless for me to attempt to give his war record, as it is well known. That he was a brave and efficient officer, we have evidence in various ways. As an instance of coolness and courage, it was said by one of his soldiers, that at one time, when surrounded by a superior force of the enemy, Major Fogg told us to load our guns, put on our bayonets, and— *Blaze Through!*

That he was a man of uncommon natural ability, as well as superior education, may be seen at once by his journals and letters, written as they were off hand, and subject to the inconveniences attending Camp Life.— His orderly books and some of his letters home have been

preserved. Among them is one written about the time of
the conviction and execution of Major Andre. showing his
feeling in regard to the matter; which he doesnt hesitate
to express in pretty strong terms.

A true copy of the original :—

" I have written repeatedly, but what or by whom, is
out of memory The last I think was concerning the Plot.
Since which Maj. Andre, Clintons Adj. Gen. has been
condemned, and was to have been executed yesterday, but
a Flag concerning him prevented. Gov. Robinson, with
two able Attornies, landed, with a letter from Arnold,
provoking and insolent, directed to ' His Excellency.'

Gen. Green received them, broke open the letter, and
returned it with due contempt ;—the purport was, that
Andre was not a Spy, but meant only to meet him within
the British Lines, but by accident blundered within our
Sentries, and had a Passport from Major Gen. Arnold, and
if he was hanged, the severest retaliation might be
expected.

What is to be done ? The Law must be satisfied. He
is a spy. And notwithstanding what Andre calls the
futile arguments, says he deserves death, by the Law and
Wage of nations, as he was taken within our Lines. On
the whole 'tis plain, he was deceived by Arnold , 'twas not
his intention to come within our Lines.   .

He is a man of elegant form, education, sense and
honor , has done no more than any friend to his cause
would. Our contracted ones speak of him as a villain
without discrimination; but such of us who profess liberal
sentiments, ache in heart, and wish for some pretext to
save him. He begs no questions may be asked, except of
his personal conduct, and will die like a *Hero* ——but,
Arnold, shocking ! shocking ! and the poor wretches in
York, who have acted as Spies for Arnold, are all in con-
finement by his information. Is not this worse than
Treason ? To say no more of him, he is a d—— per-
jured rascal.

4 o'clock, P. M. Well ! Poor Andre is gone. You have
read of martyrs, &c., but cannot figure to yourself more
fortitude in any man. He was hung in his uniform, and

shew no more discomfortation than if going to a ball.
Some of our Sensibles are almost distracted at the sight.
I am much cooled down since I saw his foolhardiness,
(alias fortitude) Am quite out of humor, and unfit to
write ; besides the long roll, calls me to parade."

At the close of the War, he returned to the Old Home,
in Kensington, to become once more a citizen of his native
town, taking an active interest in local politics ; and was
for several years a member of the New Hampshire Senate.
Here is an extract from a letter written just before his
return :

" I hope, in a few days, to be on a par with the Citizens
of the Continent, at least as a poll tax, if not Purse, when
I may feel interested in the measures of Government, and
be compelled to give my feeble voice. My first attention
will be (if I am forced to meddle with politics,) to bring
Our Illustrious Commander Chief, as near the helm of
Government as the Constitution will admit ; and rather
than he should decline a place in Government, and we be
tormented with a number of Tyrants in each State, or the
Anarchy, I would consent to submit my privileges to his
sole disposal, and that his arm be lengthened to save or
destroy at pleasure Such is my Confidence in the Recti-
tude of his heart, his Prudence to concert, and fortitude
to execute."

About that time a Society, called the Cincinnati, was
organized, to which all Officers of the Revolution were
eligible , and of which he became a member This society
was so called from Cincinnatus, a Roman Consul, out of
regard for his nobility of character, as well as simplicity
of manners.

The first President of this Society was George Washington , Gen. Knox, Secretary. The first meeting was
held in Pennsylvania, in 1784. At that time thirteen
States were represented Its object was to keep in remembrance the mutual friendships formed during their
struggle for Independance ; and cement more strongly the
ties which bound them together in sacred fellowship
The Society to endure while their lives should last, or

any of their oldest male posterity, who may be judged
worthy.   It was also a mutual benefit association.

On the 18th of December, 1785, Major Fogg was married to Lydia Hill, only daughter of Jonathan and Lydia
Hill of Cambridge.

There was quite a romance connected with their early
acquaintance ; I have often heard her tell the story :—

While he was a student at Harvard, and about seventeen
years of age, he was present at the christening of an
infant ; and he playfully remarked to a friend, that he
meant to marry her sometime ; which pledge was fulfilled
when he was thirty-five and she nineteen.

Six children were born to them,—two sons and four
daughters.   The sons, Thomas and Jeremiah, both went
West ; took up Government land ; married and settled in
Ohio   The three eldest daughters married townsmen,
well-to-do farmers. who were born, lived and died in the
good old town :—

Martha, the eldest, married Samuel Tucke, had seven
children, three sons and four daughters.

Catherine married Josiah Blake, had nine children,
five sons and four daughters

Frances married Smith Lamprey, had five children,
three sons and two daughters.

Irene, the youngest, (my mother,) married Green
Perkins, of Seabrook, had one child.   They lived in Sea-
brook several years, finally returning to the old home in
Kensington.

Major Fogg died after a short illness, in 1808, in the
house where he was born, in Kensington, aged fifty-nine
years.   We find among his descendants but few military
men, though we do not know what might have developed
had they lived in Revolutionary years   There were three,
however, who served in the Civil War, one of these having
seen service in the Mexican War.

While we do not find any especially distinguished,—no
President or Millionaire,—there were no knaves or criminals ; but just Honest and True Men and Women.

In Memoriam.

By Mrs. George Lyman Davenport, Cohasset, Mass.

Those of us who have been members of the Fogg Family Association from its very beginning at Hampton Beach, that beautiful September day, in 1902, and have looked forward each year to seeing again, at our annual gathering, pleasant acquaintances and friends, of whose very existence we might have been still ignorant were it not for this bond of descent from our common ancestor,— Samuel Fogge, are beginning to miss some warm handclasps, and must look in vain for some familiar faces.

There are others, too, who never met with us, but who were, we know, interested in our Fogg annals, and had hoped sometime to join our visible ranks, who have gone from earth, their life-work ended.

From the records furnished me by our Secretary, and from such additional information as could, in the too short time that I have been able to give to this subject, be obtained from relatives and friends of the deceased, has been derived the following necrology of the Foggs in the last three years.

Two deaths are reported in 1902 ; five in 1903 ; ten in 1904 ; five in 1905.

Ezra Dodge Fogg, born at Salem Mass., April 27, 1824, died at New Haven, Conn. Nov. 21, 1902. He was a son of Stephen Fogg, and of the sixth generation from Samuel 1, through his son, Seth 2.

James Skinner McGillivray, son of Rev. Alexander and Elisabeth (Skinner) McGillivray, was born in Nova Scotia, March 4, 1844, and died in Chelsea, Mass. Dec 23, 1902. He married Mary Ellen Fogg, of the eighth generation from Samuel 1 through his son, Daniel 2, and she survives him.

Charles Henry Fogg,—attended our first Reunion, Sept. 2, 1902, at Hampton Beach, N. H.,—he was of the eighth generation from Samuel 1, through James 2 , was born in Amesbury, Mass , Feb. 27, 1847, and died Jan. 29, 1903. He was a nephew of John H. Fogg, of Hampton ; his father, Jeremiah R. Fogg, being the elder and only brother of the latter.

Mrs. Sarah A. (Fogg) Dustin, widow of David Dustin, was born in Canaan, N. H., Sept. 19, 1828, and died at Hillsboro, N. H., April 14, 1903. She was the daughter of Samuel and Lucy (Fogg) Fogg, and a descendant on both father and mother's side in the seventh generation from Samuel 1, through James 2. She leaves two sons, Allen, of Hillsboro Bridge, N. H., and George, of Canaan, N. H.

James Leland Fogg, of the seventh generation from Samuel 1 through Seth 2, was born at Rochester, N. Y. March 20, 1845, and died in Chicago, Ill. Sept. 28, 1903, after a short illness. He was the son of James P. and Emily (Ware) Fogg. In 1863, the family moved to Chicago, where in later years they established the firm of James P. Fogg & Son, seed-merchants, which became well known through the northwest. James Leland Fogg, was afterwards connected with the Leonard Seed Co of which house he was a valued member at the time of his death

From the age of eighteen, when Chicago became his home, most of his life was spent there, with an occasional year in some other western town.

He also spent a year on a farm, then owned by his uncle Josiah Fogg, in Deerfield, Mass., "thereby following family tradition, as his mother, father, uncle, and an aunt —Miss Martha Fogg,—have at different times lived in old Deerfield St."

In 1870, he was married to Miss Elizabeth Lockwood, of Prairie Du Chien, Wis who, with their two daughters and three sons, survives him ; the eldest daughter, Emily, is married to Prof Edwin Sherwood Meade, of Hammonton, N. J.; the second is the wife of Lawrence McMasters and lives in Chicago. The two sons, Lockwood Ware and James Leland, with the youngest daughter, live with their mother in Chicago.

His sister, Miss Emily Starr Fogg, who hopes to be with us another year, says of Mr. Fogg : " In later life he was extremely deaf, and this misfortune cut him off from social life, and was a constant trial to one of his sunny, happy disposition. In all relations a loving, tender man, very dear to his own,—this tells his life's story.

Mrs. Sarah (French) Fogg, daughter of the late Joseph French, of Skowhegan, Maine, was born at that place Dec. 25, 1830. She was married Nov. 12, 1854, to Albion Kent Paris Fogg, of Cornville, Maine, who was of the 7th generation from Samuel through Seth 2. Since his death, Oct. 1, 1893, she has continued to reside in the home on the main Cornville road, which was theirs from their marriage, until her death, Oct. 29, 1903, after a year of suffering. Mrs Fogg is said to have been possessed of unusual brightness, which made her an attractive neighbor ; and to have been a shrewd manager in all domestic affairs. She leaves two daughters, Grace B. and Eliza A. Fogg.

Miss Sarah Hayden Mayer, daughter of Elisha N. and Susannah (Fogg) Mayer, and of the sixth generation from Samuel 1, through Seth 2 ; born in Braintree, Mass., March 15, 1833, died in Braintree, Nov. 24. 1903. While not a member of our Association, being quite closely confined at home of late years by ill-health, she had great interest in her ancestry, and liked to talk with relatives of her grandfather, Dr. Daniel Fogg, who came to Braintree, and established himself there in the practice of medicine, soon after the Revolution.

The house which her grandfather built, of which the front porch was modelled after that of his father, Rev. Jeremiah Fogg of Kensington, has this year been torn down by later owners, and the brass latch and handle of the front door, has been given to Miss Susannah Niles Mayer, the only sister of Miss Sarah, and is now displayed by her with pride on the front door of her present home ; she has had a knocker made to match the handle, and her only sorrow in regard to it is, that her sister is not here to enjoy it with her.

Miss Sarah taught school in Milton, more than fifty years ago ; and also, I think, in Braintree. She was an active worker in the Orthodox Cong'l Church of Braintree for many years, and was in sympathy with all good things.

Mrs. Lemuel Raymond Fogg, widow of Lemuel R. Fogg of the seventh generation, and step-mother of Charles Nelson Fogg, of the 8th generation from Samuel 1 thro' Daniel 2, died in New Gloucester, Maine, March 10, 1904.

Josiah Tilton Blake, eldest son of Josiah Tilton and Catherine (Fogg) Blake, was born in Kensington, N. H., August 26, 1812, of the sixth generation from Samuel 1 through Seth 2. His father was a farmer and sold butter and eggs in Boston. His mother, a daughter of Major Jeremiah Fogg, was born in the house built by her grand-father, Rev. Jeremiah Fogg. Mr. Blake went to Lynn, Mass., in 1836, and there learned the trade of carpenter, which he always followed He married, Jan. 10, 1841, Joanna Harris Raynes, of York, Maine, by whom he had seven children, three of whom survive him, and live in Lynn. He was all his life interested in Universalism ; and was a constant attendant at the Universalist Church in Lynn.

Seth Fogg, born April 26, 1818, at Monmouth, Maine, died at New Vineyard, Maine, April 8, 1904. He was son of Royal and Ruth (Blake) Fogg, and the only brother of Rev. John B Fogg, of Monmouth, and was of the seventh generation from Samuel 1, through Seth. He left three sons. Royal Webster, Charles Wallace, of Portland, and Elmer Winfred Fogg of New Vineyard, Maine.

Mrs Mary E (Fogg) King, born in Monmouth, Maine, Nov. 1, 1816, died May 1, 1904 ; was sister of Seth, dau. of Royal Fogg, and of the seventh generation from Samuel, through Seth.

Samuel James Fogg, born in North Hampton, N. H , May 27, 1823, died May 15, 1904. He was the son of Richard and Elisabeth (Batchelder) Fogg, and of the sixth generation from Samuel through Seth. He went to Newburyport, in 1840, when only seventeen ; and was a gardener. Mr. Fogg was almost totally blind the last few years of his life ; was patient and resigned under his affliction He attended our first reunion, and was in sympathy with Mrs. A. J. Fogg in her efforts to secure data for her memorial He leaves a daughter, Mrs. Ralph E E. Beatley, and two sons, Clarence James and George Arthur, of Newburyport.

Mrs. Almeda P. (Nichols) Fogg, born in Canaan, N. H. June 3, 1819, died May 30, 1904 She was the widow of George Wallace Fogg, who was of the sixth generation from Samuel 1, through James 2 ; leaves a son Wallace George, and a grandson George Wallace,— of Canaan.

Ireton Willard Fogg, son of Horace and Ann L. (Seabury) Fogg, and of the ninth generation from Samuel 1, through Daniel 2, was born in Greene, Maine, February 7, 1879, and died Oct. 18, 1904, at the early age of twenty-five years. He was a member of the Fogg Family Association.

Mrs. Sarah Wilcox (Adams) Fogg, born Dec. 10, 1829, died Nov. 10, 1904. She was the wife of Rev John B. Fogg, who is of the seventh generation from Samuel 1, through Seth 2. Owing to ill health, Mrs. Fogg had not attended reunions, but was a member of the Association.

Mrs. Mary E (Drake) Fogg, daughter of Samuel and Mehitabel (Pickering) Drake, of North Hampton, N H. born Jan. 9, 1832, and wife of John H Fogg of Hampton ; died Dec. 12, 1904. She was a member of the Association. Many of us remember her most pleasantly as we saw her on the Golden Wedding anniversary, Sept 2, 1902, when she stood with her husband in the garlanded bay-window, and greeted us all so kindly, just because we were of the lineage of Fogg Her face looks at us from the photographs taken that day, with a wistful happiness in its expression It is beautiful that they were not long parted.

On the last day of the year 1904, Mrs. Susan Mayer (Farnsworth) Hill, passed away. She was the daughter of Rev. James Delap and Rebecca Miller Mayer (Fogg) Farnsworth, and was born in Oxford, N. H. Nov. 17, 1827. She was of the sixth generation from Samuel 1, through Seth 2 ; her mother being a daughter of Dr. Daniel Fogg, of Braintree. Her father held several pastorates,—Oxford, N. H., Paxton, Boxboro, North Chelsea, Bridgewater, Mass. One who knew her well, writes :

" Her early life, spent in the home of her parents, gave to her naturally strong nature the firm Puritan principles upon which her character was built, and which governed and controlled all her life."

Her common school education was supplemented by that of Abbot Academy, Andover, and Lawrence Academy, Groton, Mass. She fitted herself for teaching, and pursued that vocation until her marriage, teaching in— Boxboro, Harvard, Braintree, and Bridgewater, and for a short time in Richmond, Va. Before her death, she had arranged to present a clock to the town of Bridgewater, to be placed in the village school, where she was once the teacher.

November 22, 1855, she was married to William F. Hill, of Bridgewater, where they resided until 1866, removing then to Lynn, Mass., where the longest period of her life was spent. The death of her husband, who was for twenty-seven years Deacon of the East Baptist Church, in Lynn, occurred Dec. 16, 1900.

Mrs. Hill was an earnest and faithful member of the Central Cong'l Church of Lynn, and was active in the work of the Woman's Board, and in the Sunday-school until her death. She was a charter member of the Lynn Historical Society, and of the Sons and Daughters of New Hampshire, and a much interested member of the Fogg Family Association.

Those who have known the hospitality of her home, speak of it in strongest terms. She was a loyal friend and a courageous one. From near and distant relatives, and from friends and acquaintances, comes the same warm appreciation.

Of her five children three survive her, a son and two daughters, with four grandchildren; "all of whom," as one of them has said, "rise up and call her blessed." An excellent notice of her life in the records of the Lynn Historical Society, closes with this paragraph :

"Mrs. Hill was very loyal to her Church and to her religious convictions She considered it not only a duty to *be* good but to *do* good ; and not to be weary in well-doing ; and she always did with her might, what her hand found to do. She enjoyed life, and all her years, nearly fourscore and ten, were filled with usefulness. Her friends will remember her as one, of whom it can justly be written,—She hath done what she could "

Charles Richard Fogg, a member of the Fogg Family Association, was born in North Hampton, N. H. Aug. 10, 1846, died at Newburyport, Mass., March 21, 1905. He was son of Jeremiah Batchelder and Eliza Jane (Beton) Fogg, and was of the seventh generation from Samuel 1, through Seth 2. Mr. Fogg was a member of the Historical Committee, to assist Mrs. A. J. Fogg in gathering data for the Fogg Memorial. He leaves a wife and son Herbert of Newburyport, Mass

John Henry Fogg, a member of the Fogg Family Association, was born in Hampton, N H. July 1, 1828, and died there of pneumonia, March 30, 1905, less than four months after the death of his wife. They had no children. He was the third of the six children of Abraham and Mary (Robinson) Fogg, and a descendant in the sixth generation of Samuel 1, through James 2.

He lived on the farm which had descended from the original grant from father to son, without the passing of deeds, since it was first granted to Samuel 1, as a part of his possession. James 2 was probably the first of the name to live upon it; and the house where we were welcomed in 1902, is not the original house, it being the third house erected; some timbers of the second house are preserved in the barn. But it appeals to us as no other house now standing does, as an ancestral homestead, as it in fact is, for all the descendants through James 2.

Although remote from the centre of the town, Mr. Fogg has always kept in touch with public affairs. While he has "been a practical and progressive farmer, and has kept his farm in a high state of cultivation by the most approved methods and best implements," he has repeatedly served Hampton as a Selectman, often as Chairman of the Board, and as Representative to the Legislature.

He was a zealous member of the Cong'l Church of Hampton, and has been Treasurer of the Parish for the last twenty-five years.

Since 1880, he has been a trustee of Hampton Academy. When our Association was formed, we naturally looked to him as our first President; and he filled that office with great acceptance at our recent meeting, Aug. 20, 1903.

Mrs. Sarah Waite (Shuman) Fogg, was born at Kingston, R. I. Oct. 22, 1819, and died at Wollaston, Mass., April 24, 1905. She was the widow of Abner Fogg, of the sixth generation from Samuel 1, through Seth. Mrs. Fogg leaves a son, Abner, and two daughters, Mrs. Lucinda Pierce, of Everett, and Mrs Jerome C. Hosmer, of Dorchester

Mrs. Ruth Kimball (Fogg) VanPelt, was born at Epping, N H. Sept. 19, 1846, and died at Copenhagen, N. Y. May 18, 1905. She was the wife of Samuel VanPelt, and the daughter of Nathaniel Pierce and Charlotte Ann (Twombly) Fogg, and was of the eighth generation from Samuel 1, through Seth 2, also cousin of Lewis Everett Fogg, of Keene, N. H.

Mrs. Elisabeth (Shorey) Price, was born at Industry, Maine, Feb 6, 1819, and died at Auburndale, Mass. July 12, 1905 She was the daughter of Peletiah and Sarah (Fogg) Shorey, and on her mother's side was of the 7th generation from Samuel Fogg, through Seth 2. Mrs. Price intended to join our Association a year ago, at Portland, but was prevented by illness. It has been her desire to meet with us this year ; but she has been called from earthly scenes. She is represented here today by her daughter. Mrs. Harris, and two grandaughters.

Hubbard Fogg, was born at Ossipee, N. H Oct. 12, 1829, and died at Sanford, Maine, Jan. 1, 1903.

He was son of James Fogg, and Hannah (Hubbard) Fogg, who was a very successful teacher of common schools in Ossipee, N H. and Parsonfield, Maine, and the grandson of Dea. Seth Fogg, of the First Free Baptist Church at Ossipee, and was of the seventh generation from Samuel 1 through Seth 2.

Hubbard Fogg was appointed a member in 1902, of the Historical Committee, to assist Mrs. A. J. Fogg in gathering data for her Fogg Memorial. He began teaching in 1848, and taught in Sanford, Saco, Me., Dover, N. H., and Boston Reform School at Deer Island.

Mr. Fogg leaves a daughter, Mrs. Fred A. Brown, of Portland, and four sons, Willis A. of Malden, Mass., George Herbert, of Chicago, Newton H , Newell T. of Springvale, Maine.

William Williams Fogg, born at Brooks, Maine, Oct. 12 1845, died at Bangor, Maine, Dec 8, 1904, son of John Hamilton and Esther (Davis) Fogg, and eighth in descent from Samuel 1 through his son Daniel 2 Mr Fogg was a merchant in Bangor, served in the Civil War, where he lost his health. He died of an apoplectic shock, six hours after attack. Left a widow ; no children.

Only one of those whose names are here given, attained the ripe age of either of the sons of Samuel, yet while his four sons lived to be over ninety, there were three others who died while mere children,—so the average may be much the same

Many later lives may be richer in many ways than those of the dwellers in Hampton, but we owe much to our "forbears," there by the great ocean, for the quiet strength of character they bequeathed to us.

The Antiquity Interesting.

Read by the writer, ALVBN H. FOGG, Rockland, Maine.

The Foggs in England, of which those in New England are descendants, signify great age ; the antiquity interesting.

These matters are found and recorded in that *Domesday Book*, said to be the finest of European records Compiled by commissioners appointed by William the Conqueror, in the year 1086 Also revised in the year 1273 ; here again the Foggs are found as land owners Kent county is the most solid part of England ; here many families took most solid hold Of course some branches have run out ; others have continued

The life of Katherine Parr perhaps will serve to illustrate She was the Queen Consort of King Henry VIII. She descended from a long-line of Foggs, briefly stated, that noble woman maintaining Court life, through her diplomacy she not only escaped the fate of his other wives, but she had done much to restrain the many bad moves of which King Henry the VIII was noted

After his death, she married Lord Seymore, the Uncle of Edward VI Katherine died in the year 1548

During the Norman Conquest, from 1017 to 1042, Eng-

land and Ireland were ruled by three successive Danish
Kings. As a result of this, war traditions reveal that the
Foggs in England fought their own blood

Says the family writers, they were known among the
Vicking or Jute Tribe before they were known in England
or before the English lauguage was spoken A warlike
people, who in common with others, were a menace to the
Southern countries,—notably England, Ireland and the
north of France. A people who inhabited what is now
known as Denmark, a land of *fog*. A people who in early
days were exposed to cold, wet and dreary privations ;—
stamped into their natures that deep seriousness contin-
uing to the present day.

The Northmen were a bold, adventurous, enduring
people. History reveals that they led a wild life As the
eldest son inherited the estate, the younger sons were
engaged in war and voyages of discovery of a number of
lands, among them our own New England from the year
1001 to 1007, or about five hundred years prior to the
discovery by Columbus ; yet nothing grew out of it.

Samuel Fogg, the first parent we know, of Exeter,
England, no record of any other. sailed* from Yarmouth.
April 8, 1620, in the ship *Arobell*, a name known and
cherished by the older members of the family. Among
his fellow voyagers, he had a goodly number of prominent
people ; some of whom were wealthy men and women,
well educated. leaving behind them good homes. They
were coming to New England in order to do something.
America had been discovered 138 years, yet little or nothing had been done in behalf of colonization , but in that
memorable year, 1630, in the Western horizon, hitherto
unknown, appeared a ray of light.

Among the ship's company was John Winthrop, that
noble pioneer, the first Governor of Massachusett's Bay
Colony. The ship arrived in Salem sixty-five days later,
—a colony then comprising but few people.

There were previously sent out people, the number not
stated, to erect suitable shelterings, preparatory to the

---

* No proof of this can be found.—Mrs. A. J. FOGG.

coming of the Puritan fathers and mothers. Instead, upon their arrival, they found but a few small huts. That first autumn and winter, as the result of exposure and privations, about 200 precious souls sickened and died in the solitude of the New England wilderness. Some aid was provided by the Plymouth Colony ; yet hard were the losses of those people to the Massachusetts Bay Colony.

In early Colonial history, one may read the workings of the grateful hearts, contemplative minds, who the first season founded Salem, Charlestown, Cambridge, Watertown, Roxbury, Dorchester, Boston, then called Shawmut or the Three Hills,—founded late that season.

Thus commenced the settling of New England, except a feeble attempt by the Plymouth Colony.

In the ship *Arobell* came to New England the first germ of religious toleration In the now city of Providence, in the year 1636, was founded a full measure of human rights, a system that never dies ; besides they contended that the Sovereign of England had no right to deprive the Indians of their hunting ground, giving them nothing in return, who were ever the white man's friend who advocated their cause.

* * Samuel Fogg, as it was then common among others, did not settle in Massachusetts. In his wanderings of eight years, as if to escape some of the entanglements prevailing in the new world, he journeyed northward, along the Atlantic coast, to Hampton, in the year 1638.— He there hewed himself a home, whose primeval forest and broad acres, himself, his sons and their sons labored and stood sentinel over eight generations.

Samuel at the age of thirty-nine, married Anna Shaw ; she bore him two living sons.

His second wife, Mary Page, bore him two sons,— Seth and James

There were seven Samuels down to seventy years ago

Samuel the second lived 107 years ; Daniel 95 , Seth 90; and James 92.

Samuel 2, married Mary Marston in 1666 ; he settled on his father's estate , subsequently moved to New Jersey

Samuel 3d, born 1756, and wife,—she who was Ruth

Lane, born 1762, migrated from New Hampshire in the year 1805, including 15 children,—my father then a babe ; they journeyed and settled in Cornville, Maine. Children, seventeen ; eight of whom became fathers, and eight were mothers. The next to the youngest son was accidentally scalded to death, in early life Grandchildren originating—127 ; but from Daniel and Hannah (Libbey) Fogg, who settled in Eliot, from that branch the most of the Foggs originated

There are in Portsmouth and vicinity a few colored people by the name of Fogg, said to be the descendants of Fogg slaves,—the name they adopted in recent times.

Samuel Fogg and his descendants ;—early descendants whom we have met to commemorate. It gives me pleasure to say, they have done much to mold the history of our Country. The daughters long ago were engaged in the activities of life ; with the hand-loom clothed the world ; while the sons were engaged in the Colonial Wars In the battles of Quebec, at Louisburg, in the War of the Revolution, they were engaged. In the Wars of more recent date they were engaged True to the records of their ancestry, they fought and bled ; they have done their duty.

Do what you can for others, as well as for yourself ! In this respect continue to emulate the lives of our great FAMILY, who from authentic record have maintained their identity nearly a thousand years.

One word more . We are living in a country having no independent name of its own. I think our Government should by a Congressional enactment, discard the word *America*, and substitute in thoughtful remembrance of the achievements won by the great Discoverer,—yes, that genial sentence .

THE UNITED STATES OF COLUMBIA.

A Dissertation on Heraldry.

Prepared and read at Boston by Mrs. A. J. FOGG

Heraldry may be defined, "The art of blazoning, assigning and marshalling coat armour," or, more particularly, the art of explaining in proper terms, all that relates or appertains to the bearing of Arms, Crests, Badges, Quarterings, and other hereditary marks of honor.

The origin of badges and emblems may certainly be traced to the earliest times; but while it may be admitted that in the ancient world, warlike nations bore on their shields and standards distinguishing devices, it is not clear that ever Heraldry can be traced to a more remote period than the twelfth, or at farthest, the eleventh century. Numerous tombs existed, of persons of noble blood, who died before the year 1000. Yet there is not an instance known of one with a heraldic bearing

The word *Heraldry*, is derived from the German Herr, a host, or army; and Held, a champion. And the term *Blazon*, has most probably its origin in the German word, blazen, "to blow the horn" Whenever a new Knight appeared at a tournament, the herald sounded the trumpet, and as the competitors attended with closed visor, it was his duty to explain the bearing of the shield or coat armour belonging to each.

At first, armorial bearings were probably like surnames, assumed by each warrior at his free will and pleasure, to distinguish himself and followers from others

The earliest Heraldic documents that have been handed down, are the—

Roll of Arms, made between the years 1240 and 1245; it contained the names and the arms of the Barons and Knights of the reign of King Henry III;

The Roll of Arms of King Edward 2nd, made between the years 1308 and 1314; is divided into counties, and comprised the names and arms of about 1160 persons;

And still another Roll appears to have been compiled between the years 1337 and 1350, which was most comprehensive, embracing the Arms of all the Peers and Knights in England, arranged in the following order.— First: the King, the Earls, the Barons Second: the

Knights, under their respective counties. Third : The great Personages who lived in earlier times. ·

In the reign of Henry V, a proclamation was issued, prohibiting the use of Heraldic ensigns, to all who could not show an original and valid right, except "those who had borne arms at Agincourt." But, despite the royal ordinance, abuses continued to such an extent, they gave rise in the early part of the sixteenth century to the Heraldic Visitations, documents of high authority and value.

Royal commissions were issued under the Great Seal, to the two Provincial Kings of Arms, authorizing and commanding each, by himself or duputy, to visit the whole of his provinces, and summon those who bore, or assumed to bear arms, and were styled Esquires, to produce their authority for bearing or using the same. All persons who can deduce descent from an ancestor whose armorial ensigns have been acknowledged in any one of these visitations, are entitled to carry those arms by right of inheritance.

Nobles bore their arms, charged upon their shield, which is also designated the field or escutcheon. The shield, when in actual use, was held by the Knight in front of him, and in a representation of a coat of arms, that part of the shield which occurs on the left side is called the Dexter, and that on the right the Sinister.

The colors common to shields, or their bearings, are called tinctures, and are of seven different kinds; five colors and two metals, viz gold ; arjent, silver or white ; azure, blue ; gules, red ; vert, green ; purpure, purple ; and sable, black.

Charges are the various figures depicted on shields, by which the bearers are distinguished one from another. All charges are either proper or common. The proper charges are those which particularly belong to the Art of Heraldry, and are of ordinary use therein ; hence they are styled Ordinances. Among the proper charges is the Fess, crossing the shield horizontally. and emblematic of the military girdle worn around the body over the armor.

Differences, marks of cadency are the distinctions used

to indicate the various branches or cadets of one family, and are found on the shield directly under the helmet.— The eldest son, during the lifetime of his father, bears a Label; the second son, a Crescent; the third, a Mullet; the fourth, a Martlett; the fifth, an Annulet; and so on

The Crest,—yields in honor to none of the heraldic insignas; and derives its name from Crista, a cockscomb; and was deemed a greater mark of nobility than the Coat armor. For the latter, the Noble would succeed by birth; but to obtain the former, he must be a Knight in actual service. The Crest was the emblem that served when the banner was rent assunder, and the shield broken, as a rallying point for Knight's followers, and a distinguishing mark of his own prowess.

As early as the year 1101, a Seal of Philip, Count of Flanders, represents him with a Crest; but at that period and for a century and a half after, few of lesser degree than Sovereigns or Commanders in the wars, ventured to carry this mark of distinction.

After the institution, however, of the Order of the Garter, the Knights of that illustrious Order, adopted Crests; and the practice soon became so general, that these emblems were assumed indiscriminately by all those who considered themselves legally entitled to Coat Armor.

Originally Crests were carved in light wood, or made of boiled leather, passed into a mould, in the form of some animal, real or fictious, and were placed over the belmet, with the Torse Wreath or Bandean between, which was formed by two pieces of silk, "twisted together by the Lady who chose the bearer for her Knight." The tinctures of the Torse, are always those of the principal metal and color of the arms; and it is the rule in delineating the Torse, that the first coil shall be of the metal, and the last coil of the color of which the achievement is constituted.

Crests have sometimes been confounded with Badges, —a distinct device, intended to distinguish the retainers of certain great noblemen, and wrought or sewn upon their liveries This was held in high esteem, until the reign of Queen Elisabeth,—when the last brilliant relic of the feudal system,—the joust, tournament, and all their paraphernalia, fell into disuse.

The Motto is a word, saying or sentence, which gentlemen carried in a scroll under the Arms, and sometimes over the Crest. It was considered the watchword of the Camp, and its use can be traced to a remote period. It is asserted they came into use during the reign of Henry III. Be this as it may, their general usage may be accurately dated from the institution of the Order of the Garter ; for after the celebrated event, they became very general, and daily gained in favor. During the wars of Henry V, VI, and VIII, innumerable mottoes graced the shields of the warriors. And in the courtly days of Queen Elisabeth, devices were especially fashionable. Mottoes were taken, changed, relinquished, when, and as often as the bearer thought best.

The Helmet or Casque is varied in shape in different ages and countries The most ancient is the simplest, composed of iron, of a shape fitted to the head, and flat upon the top, with an aperture for light. This is styled the Norman Helmet, and appears on very old seals, attached to the Gorjet, a separate piece of armor that covered the neck. The Helmet is placed immediately above the escutcheon and supports the Torse on which is the Crest.

The Mantle is from a French word, Manteau, and served as a protection, (being spread over and pendant from the Helmet,) to repel the extremity of wet, cold and heat, and withal to preserve the accoutrements from rust.

Sept. 1, 1905 :

The company met with Mrs. Adna J. Fogg, and visited places of historic interest in Boston ; one of these localities was the Fogg Art Museum at Harvard,—a monument indeed to the name.

The various offices for the year, were filled with names which grow more and more universal, as the Associations are repeated :—

Honorary President :—
    Rev. John B. Fogg, Monmouth, Maine.

President :
    Mrs. George Lyman Davenport, Cohasset, Mass.

Vice Presidents :
    Mrs. James Skinner McGillivany, Boston.
    George Frederick Shedd, Nashua, N. H.
    Almon Hayes Fogg, Houlton, Maine.

Executive Committee :
    Mrs. Frank A. Fogg, Laconia, N. H.
    Mrs. Willis Allen Fogg, Malden, Mass.
    Mrs. Emery A. R. Fogg Ayers, East Boston, Mass.
    Mrs. Vanrice A. Stephens, Boston.
    Mrs. Charles Augustus Hillard, Lynn, Mass.
    Mrs. Frank Prescott Fogg, Dorchester, Mass.
    Mrs. Lewis Everett Fogg, Keene, N. H.
    Mrs. Ella Fogg Hasty, Limerick, Maine.

Secretary and Treasurer :
    Mrs. Adna J. Fogg, Boston.

(next page :)

The Secretary gave the following records, or "items," which are of both value and interest

We have on our books, two hundred and twenty-one members.   Of these,—

Thirty-three are Charter members.

First Reunion, September 2, 1902.

    40 became members 1902 3.
    60 became members 1903-4.
    40 became members 1904-5
    44 became members 1905-6.

Thirty-three members have paid yearly dues		4 years.
Thirty-four	" "	3 years
Forty-four	" "	2 years.
Ten	" "	1 year

Our Registration Book shows

    One hundred and ninety-four registered at the First Reunion, September 2, 1902, Hampton Beach.

    One hundred and ninety-seven registered at the Second Reunion, August 20, 1903 Hampton Beach

    One hundred and eighty-four registered at the Third Reunion, August 21, 1904, Portland, Maine

    One hundred and sixty-two registered at the Fourth Reunion, August 31, 1905, Boston

The Youngest Charter Member, is—

    Forrest Glenn Fogg, Boston, born September 26, 1887, son of A J Fogg ; and descended in the ninth generation from Samuel the First through his Fourth son, James

The Oldest Charter Member, was—

    Rev John Blake Fogg, born at Monmouth, Maine, February 14, 1825, (now deceased,) descended in the seventh generation from Samuel the 1st, through his third son Seth

The oldest male member of our Association, is—

    Hiram Hayes Fogg, Bangor, Maine ;
born at Milton Pond, N. H. September 4, 1824 ;
descended in the sixth generation from Samuel the 1st,
through his second son, Daniel

The oldest female member of our Association, is—
Mrs. Hannah Higgins Fogg Boobar, San Francisco ,
born at Bowdoinham, Maine, July 20, 1823;
descent either from Samuel or Seth,—sons of Samuel 1st

The youngest female member of our Association, is—
Blanche Taylor Fogg, Laconia, N. H.;
born at Derry, N. H. Dec. 17, 1892 ;
daughter of Frank Appleton Fogg ; and a descendant in
the eighth generation from Samuel the 1st, through his
third son, Seth.

The youngest member of our Association is .
Lawrence W. Fogg, Hartford, Conn ,
born November 16, 1900 ,   .
son of Elmer Harris Fogg, and descended in the ninth
generation from Samuel the first, through his 3d son Seth.

The oldest one (to my knowledge,) of the name
Fogg, today, in New Hampshire, is Stephen Fogg,—
living in Sandwich ,
Born in Sandwich, N. H Dec. 31, 1818 ,
descended in the sixth generation from Samuel the first,
through his fourth son, James.

(next page .)

Of our Charter Members, —
        three have passed away :

Mrs. Susan Thayer Hill, Lynn, Mass. 1904.
Mrs John Blake Fogg, Monmouth, Maine, 1904.
Rev. John Blake Fogg, Monmouth, Maine, 1905

Three of our Members have finished their work here
below :—

Charles Richard Fogg, Newburyport, Mass. 1905.
Ireton W. Fogg, Greene, Maine, 1904
John Henry Fogg, Hampton, N H., 1905.

We have received
            since our first Reunion, 1902,— $317 57.
The Total Expenses— $295 18.

These last pages, 102-3-4, are from a paper issued by the
        Secretary and Treasurer, Mrs. Adna J. Fogg.

Fogg Family Association. 5th Reunion.

HAMPTON BEACH, NEW HAMPSHIRE.

AUGUST 31,—SEPTEMBER 1, 1906.

With ideal weather, and the best of good will and friendliness, the Fogg Family of America, assembled for the *Fifth time* at—

Picnic Hall, Casino Building, Hampton Beach, N. H.

The cars brought large numbers of the Family to the Beach ; and the early hours were spent in registry and renewing acquaintance.

The literary exercises were called for, at one o'clock, by the President of the Association,—Willis Allen Fogg,— of Malden, Mass , who gave an interesting introductory address :—

The Cordial Greeting.

By the President, WILLIS ALLEN FOGG.

It is indeed a pleasure to greet such a gathering, and to extend to all here assembled a most cordial welcome to this the Fifth Annual Reunion of the Fogg Family of America.

We are welcomed here to day by the outreached arms of the tossing sea, and by the sweet music of the waves upon the shore.

Ex-Gov. John D. Long, has appropriately said on a somewhat similar occasion · "Enough if I touch the chord that is vibrating in each of your breasts, the electric fluid flashing back through the past, opening up all their vistas, peopleing them with the familiar faces and scenes of childhood, reminding us that youth,—though the years pass, though age comes, though the locks whiten, is eternal in the spirit, and shall endure forever in the memory."

In memory of the dead, in honor of the living, and as an example to our children, we have assembled here to picture the romance and virtue of our ancestors

Is it any wonder we should enjoy meeting together at these Annual Reunions, to consider questions pertaining to our early ancestry, and talk over the old days when we were boys and girls at home, possibly on the farm down in Maine, or up here in New Hampshire, the birthplace of the old home week.

What a blessing it is to have had the fostering care of a sweet and tender and loving mother Such a memory brings joy and gladness to our hearts This Nation owes much to the worthy women of the land, who trained their children in the fundamental principles of good citizenship

Those of us present, who attended a former Reunion here, will recall with pleasure the brief visit we made upon the late Mr. and Mrs John Fogg, on the day of their Golden Wedding, at the original home of Samuel Fogg, and their kindness and cordial greeting.

In our imagination, we can see Mr and Mrs Fogg standing in front of the old homestead, with us gathered in a large family circle on the spacious lawn, and we can almost hear the well-chosen words of introduction and good cheer, offered by our late and beloved President, John Blake Fogg, of Monmouth, Maine, as he addressed the 7th or 8th generation of Samuel Fogg, upon that historical ground of our forefathers

Emerson has truly said · " It is long ere we discover how rich we are Our history we are sure, is quite tame We have nothing to write, nothing to infer. But our wiser years still run back to the despised recollections of childhood, and always we are fishing up some wonderful article out of that pond."

As you well know the name of *Fogg* is of great age in England And those who bear it are found as land owners in the Book of the hundred rolls, prepared under the direction of King Edward the First, in the year 1273

And at an earlier date the name is found in the Domesday Book, compiled by commissioners appointed by— William the Conqueror, in the year 1086, only twenty years after the Conquest of England by the Normans

Samuel Fogg, our early ancestor, settled in Hampton about the year 1638 His first wife was Anne Shaw, whom he married Oct 12, 1652, when he was 39 years of age. She died in the year 1661. By this marriage he had four sons and one daughter ; but only the eldest and youngest sons lived to grow to manhood : Samuel born 1653, Daniel born 1660.

Samuel Fogg married for his second wife, Mary Page ; a daughter of Robert Page, who was a large land owner, and member of the General Court. By this marriage he had two sons, Seth and James, and a daughter, Hannah. The four sons of Samuel Fogg lived to the remarkable ages,—Samuel, 107, Daniel 95, Seth 90, James 92.

Samuel Fogg the 1st, made a wise choice in selecting a home in this part of the country. In those early days the rivers and sea were the principal highways, and an important source of food supply He little dreamed what a famous resort this region was destined to become. Today the whole seacoast between Hampton River, N H and Ogunquit Harbor, Me. offers many and varied attractions to the summer visitor.

Portsmouth, (in later years a home of the Foggs,) was throughout the colonizing period, and up to the Revolutionary War, one of the most important seaports in the new world. It was the residence of the Royal Governors up to the time the Royal authority was overthrown.

It was near here, it is claimed, at Fort Constitution, in Colonial days called Fort William, at the northeast extremity of Newcastle, that the first overt act of armed rebellion against the authority of the crown occurred.

The Fort was captured by a party of men, led by Capt Thompson and John Langdon of Portsmouth,—the latter who was afterwards elected Governor of New Hampshire

The history of the United States is rich in romance and patriotism of a people, who by their loyalty and faithful performance of duty, while at home or on the battlefield, have made it possible for us to enjoy an unprecidented degree of prosperity, such as the world has never known.

Frederick Schlegel says, that God has revealed Himself

in four ways :—In the Scripture, in Nature, in Conscience, and in Human History.

At the close of the President's introductory and historic words, the little soulful hymn, " Blest be the tie that binds," was sung.—Miss Marion Shedd, Haverhill, Ms., piano accompanist.

Then followed the Paper entitled, "Original Diary of Jeremy Fogg," born at Scarboro, Maine, January 11, 1744, read by his great-grandaughter, Mrs. George F. Shedd, of Nashua, New Hampshire The Diary contained quaint and odd sayings :—

Diary of Jeremy Fogg.

Read at the Fifth Reunion, by Mrs. George F. Shedd.

Preliminary Remarks :

Mr. President, and Members of the Fogg Family Association :

Before reading the Diary of Jeremy Fogg, I want to tell you simply who he was. I trust you will pardon me if in doing so, I repeat words you have heard before. For in the busy strife of every day life, we are apt to forget things to which our attention is called but once a year :

Samuel Fogg, the imigrant ancestor and progenator of most, if not all, who bear the name, was an early settler in Hampton.

In the year 1638, the General Court granted the petitioners liberty to settle. Samuel Fogg bought the farm from Christo Hussey, which until recently remained in the family, passing by inheritance from one generation to another

Samuel Fogg's fourth son, born June 19, 1660, was named *Daniel*, and I meet here today, many wearing the badges bearing that name.

Daniel Fogg was a blacksmith by trade. He married Hannah Libbey, About 1680, he removed to (Black Point) Scarboro, Maine. He had a family of nine children, five sons and four daughters. He died in Eliot, Me. June 9, 1755, aged 95 years.

One of his sons, born April 12, 1694, in Scarboro, Me.,

was named Daniel, and in later years was known as Capt.
Daniel He married Anne Hanscom, of Eliot, Maine,
July 30, 1715.

Samuel, their first son, born June 1, 1716, in Eliot, was
named for his Great-grandfather. About the year 1722,
Capt. Daniel Fogg removed with his family to Scarboro.
Samuel Fogg married Rachel ———, Jan. 27, 1743, and
their first son, born June 11, 1744, in Scarboro, was named
Jeremy.

I hold in my hand the Original Diary,—worn and yellow
with age,—penned with his own hand, which I will now
read .

[Extracts from the Diary]

Mr. Daniel Fogg, my Great Grand Father was Born in
the Year, 1660, and Died in Kittery,* June the 9th Day,
1775, aged 95 years.

Capt. Daniel Fogg, my Grand Father, was Born April
the 12th day, 1694.

Mrs Anna Fogg, my Grand Mother, was Born August
the 16th, 1694.

Mrs. Anna Fogg, my Grand Mother, Died April ye 15th
1775, Aged 80 years & 8 months.

Capt. Daniel Fogg, my grand Father, Died November
the 30th, 1785, aged 88 years & 7 months & 18 days.

Mr Samuel Fogg, their first Son, and my Father, was
Born June ye first day, 1716   And died October the 30,
1798, Aged 82 years, 4 months, 19 days.

My Aunt Anna Fogg, their first Daughter, was Born
Feb'y the 16th 1718, married August 24, 1738, John Libbee.

My Aunt Hannah Fogg, their second Daughter, was
Born Novemb'r ye 12th day 1719, married to Wm Hopty,
Septm. ye 8th, 1748.

My Uncle Ruben Fogg, their Second Son, was Born
June ye first day 1772, married May ye 15th 1744 to Mar-
gret Elder.

The Diary, a book evidently of solid value, contains
pages of family births, marriages, &c.; but as they will be

* Now Eliot, Maine.

included in Mrs. Fogg's forthcoming Memorial, we need not insert them here. Of his immediate relatives, he adds the names and dates of his Aunt Mary, who married Geo. Hanscom ; Aunt Keturah, who married Elisha Hanscom ; Aunt Esther, who married Elisha Libbey ; Aunt Rhoda, who died early ; Uncle Daniel who married Sarah Scott, of Machias, Maine.

A vocal solo was rendered by Clarence H. Fogg, of Newburyport, Mass., which merited an encore.

After the solo was a historical paper on the *Fogg Family Lore*, written by John Livingston Wright, Boston, Mass., and read by Mrs. Adna J. Fogg. Livingston Wright is the great-grandson of Dea. Seth Fogg, who was born in Ossipee, N. H. in 1766.

Fogg Family Lore.

JOHN LIVINGSTON WRIGHT.
Read by Mrs. Adna J. Fogg.

One can seldom visit a Family Reunion, without being reminded at some time or other during the session, of what the famous lawyer and statesman, William M. Evarts, said, when called upon at a banquet of the Potter Family, of which he was an honored offshoot. There had been some pretty fulsome landing of various Potters, and the usual tendency had been well exhibited, of piling it on sweet and thick, regarding the good points and graciously sliding over the peccadilloes that stern critics might have dug up. Anticipating a masterpiece from the eloquent Evarts, the company did not call upon him until several inconsequential and long-winded wights had had their say.

Late in the evening, Evarts arose, glanced mischievously around him, and in his own indescribably humorous way, observed :

" Well I don't know as there's much left for me to say, except that I might quote the Biblical phrase, "Oh, Lord, thou art the clay, but we're the potters. (Potters.)"

However, in this paper, I do not intend to exaggerate or glorify any especial section of the Fogg Family, but mean to present an impartial and accurate synopsis of its origin and history in general.

As a literary man, I may say, that many times in common with others of the craft, I have distracting difficulty in trying to sift historical fact from tradition and folk lore. Whatever the inaccuracies of this paper may be, I assure you, that I have sought to offer only that which can be depended upon as reasonably trustworthy. You are well aware that in family history, recollection usually goes back no farther than to a sort of vague description of a grand parent, a traditionally story or two, and from that the path swift leads into a baffling mist of "guess so's." and probably, into "don't exactly know's."

If I shall have, here and there, set forth a fact that may be of interest or help to other investigators, so that one day there shall come forth a worthy and exhaustive Genealogy of the Fogg Family, the object of this essay will have obtained.

Properly proud of the fact that I have Fogg blood in my veins, and that, too, of so truly a good man as Dea. Seth Fogg, of Ossipee, New Hampshire, I have long had a deep interest in all that attaches to the history of the name. and what I present here, are bits that have been gathered from a multitude of book and record authority to which has been added considerable, gathered by word of mouth from aged members of the Fogg Family. '

A family noted for its interest and endowment of institutions of learning, and which, in this country, first established itself in New Hampshire, near the Maine line, is the Fogg Family, of traditionally and presumably Welsh origin, as the very name itself suggests; it is also found in Denmark, so it is said.

Since 1630, when the first of the name settled in this country, there have been distributed over America, descendants today estimated at fully three thousand

The leaders of this Family have been characterized by an especial zeal for religion, and the endowment of schools, and in England and the United States are several illustrations of the family distinction. For instance,—

there is the FOGG MUSEUM OF ART, at Harvard University, which was erected to perpetuate the memory of William Hayes Fogg, and presented to the University by his wife.

Rev. Jeremiah Fogg, of Kensington, N, H, of the third generation in this country, was noted for his learning, and was a graduate of Harvard University. His sons, Major Jeremiah, and Dr. Daniel Fogg, were heroes of the Revolutionary War.

One of the most noted of the family was Lady Catherine Parr, the last wife of the much married Henry VIII, of England

The first Fogg to settle in America was Samuel Fogge, who arrived at Salem, Mass., in 1630, from Exeter, England, though some claim he was born in Wales. He went to Exeter, N H. in 1638, and shortly afterwards settled in the town of Hampton, N. H. and established what was destined to be the headquarters of the Fogg Family in America.

October 12, 1652, he married Ann Shaw, of Hampton. They were parents of four sons and one daughter. Two of the sons died in infancy. Their youngest child was Daniel, who eventually settled at Eliot, (Kittery,) Maine, and established the branch of the Fogg family that comes from Eliot. The sons of Samuel and Ann Shaw were :

Samuel who lived to be 107 years old, was the oldest ;

Daniel 1st, died in infancy ;

Daniel 2d, was the youngest son, and lived to be 90 yrs;
The second wife of Samuel Fogg was Mary Page, of Hampton. She had two sons, and a daughter Hannah. The sons were Seth and James.

From Seth, is descended Deacon Seth Fogg, who settled at Ossipee, where, in 1798, he bought 100 acres of land for *one shilling*. It is from Deacon Seth Fogg that the writer of this paper is descended,—being his great-grandson

These sons and daughters of Samuel 1st, settled in the territory adjacent to Hampton,—such as Kensington, Exeter, Eliot, (Kittery,) and Scarboro. Thus, wherever in the North American continent, you strike a Fogg, the ancestry will trace back to one of these New Hampshire or Maine settlements.

As illustrative of the presumed Welsh origin of the Foggs, it is interesting to cite that in several of the old deeds, the name is spelled with the true Welsh style,— Ffogge.

Now, of these five living children of Samuel Fogg, there was the following issue : Daniel married Hannah Libbey, and moved to Kittery, (now Eliot,) about 1690. His oldest son, Daniel, was born about 1687, and settled in Scarboro, Me. His second child, Mary, married Dr. Burke, of Kittery. His third child, John, settled in Scarboro. His fourth child, Hannah, married G. Rogers, of Kittery, (Eliot.) His fifth child, Joseph, was born about 1695, and settled in Scarboro. His sixth child, Rebecca. married Mr. Pillsbury. His seventh child, Seth, settled in Scarboro. His eighth child, Sarah, married Dr. Hanscom. His ninth child, James, born 1702, settled in Kittery, (Eliot,) and married Elisabeth Fernald, in 1730.

This Daniel Fogg, the son of Samuel 1st, died at Eliot in 1750, aged 95, (and his grave has an ancient stone)

Seth Fogg, the third son of Samuel 1st, had four sons, Abner, Samuel, Ebenezer and Jeremiah.

Jeremiah, the youngest child, was the one who became so noted as "the learned Fogg," and was the congregational minister at Kensington, N. H· He was a graduate of Harvard University, and became widely known as a man of learning.

Abner Fogg, the son of Seth 2. the son of Samuel 1st, had three sons, Abner, Seth and Samuel ; and three daughters, Elisabeth, Bethiah and Abigail. This latter Seth, (son of Abner,) was the father of Deacon Seth Fogg, of Ossipee, a man who was almost as prominent in the territory, in and around Ossipee. for wisdom and uprightness of character, as was his famous relative, the Rev'd Jeremiah, of Kensington.

The other children of Seth, the son of Abner, were,— Sarah, Mary, Jane, Simon and Abner.

Deacon Seth Fogg, of Ossipee, had four daughters, Polly, Betsey, Ann and Leucadia ; and four sons, Daniel, Nathan, James and Amasa.

James Fogg, the third son of Dea. Seth Fogg of Ossipee married Hannah Hubbard, of Limington, Me. They had six sons and three daughters. The sons were Daniel, Moses, John, James and Hubbard. [The latter died not long ago, at Sanford, Me.]

The daughters were—Ruth, Hannah and Elisabeth; the latter is the only surviving member of the family. She married Mr. Burke, and lives in Somerville, Mass

Like the Sir John and Francis Fogge of Old England, we find in New England several educational institutions, besides those already mentioned, that carry on the work in which the ancestors in Old England were so deeply interested : Berwick, Me. has an Academy, endowed by a Fogg. Eliot, Me. is to have a Fogg Memorial Library. In connection with Libraries, it may be noted, that William Fogg 5th, of Eliot, was one of Maine's most prominent Genealogists.

Besides the Foggs, already mentioned, who have attained distinction, or been of prominence in their country, may be noted the following :—

Archdeacon Peter Parry Fogg. He was educated at Oxford, England, which country is his native land, and afterwards studied in Germany. Since 1871, he has been Archdeacon of George, and is located at George, Cape of Good Hope. He was made Vicar General of St Helena, in 1899. He is the third son of J. Barrett Fogg, of England.

Thomas Biddle Fogg, of Toledo, Ohio, is Vice President of the Toledo Terminal Railway Co ; he was born in 1861, at Hancock Bridge, Salem Co., New Jersey.

George Gilman Fogg, of New Hampshire, was a United States Senator, and was appointed by President Lincoln, as United States Minister to Switzerland. He was born at Meredith, N. H. in 1815, graduated from Dartmouth College, 1839, and practiced Law, at Gilmanton, some years. In 1866, he was appointed United States Senator from New Hampshire. He was the son of David and Hannah Gilman (Vickery) Fogg.

William Perry Fogg, author and traveller, was born in Exeter, N. H. 1826 ; son of Josiah Fogg and grandson of Josiah Fogg, and in the 7th generation from Samuel 1st. His grandfather was Lieut Colonel, under Gen. Sullivan, in the Revolutionary War. Mr. Fogg resides in Roselle, New Jersey. He was President of the Coxton Book Co. of New York. He edited the Cleveland Herald from 1870 to 1880. He made a two years tour of the world, starting in 1871. He is the author of ''Westward Round the World,'' 1871 ; and ''Arabistan,'' 1875.

The Foggs have already been referred to with regard to their interest in peace and religion. Now let us glance at their name in the arts of War · An examination of the records of the early Indian Wars of the Colonies, show frequent mention of the name of *Fogg*, as do also those of the Revolution, the War of 1812, and the Civil War.

In King William's War, 1689-1698, the names of James and Samuel Fogg are found as those of valiant soldiers. Benoni Fogg, of Searbow, served in Capt James Davis' Co. in Queen Anne's War, 1702-13. In Lieut Joseph Swett's Co. was James Fogg, a sergeant

The prominence in the Revolution of Major Jeremiah and Dr Daniel Fogg, of Kensington, has already been noted. Another is Lieut John Fogg.

In the War of 1812, Abraham Fogg served in Capt. Philip Towle's Co. of Col. Lovering's N. Hampshire Reg.

In Queen Anne's war, Seth Fogg, of Hampton, served at Fort William and Mary, from Jan. 1, to July 15, 1708.

In King George's War, 1744 to 1749, Samuel Fogg of Hampton, served with Capt. Nat Drake's Co.

In the French and Indian War, 1754 to 1763, Capt. Abner Fogg, commanded the 5th Co. of Horsemen.

In the assault on Louisberg, under the command of Col. William Pepperell, was Capt. Daniel Fogg.

In the War of 1812, there served in Capt. Quimby's Co Daniel, John, and Oren Fogg, of Sandwich, N. H.— Sherburne Fogg was also a member of Capt. Enoch Quimby's Co Serving in Capt. Stephen Clark's Co. was Samuel Fogg, of Exeter, N. H.

Soldiers in the War of the Revolution included David and Seth Fogg, who served in Capt. Simon Marston's Co.

In the War of 1812, with Capt. Nath'l Gilman's Co. was David Fogg.

In giving a word to the particular Fogg from whom the the writer is descended, namely, Dea. Seth Fogg, of Ossipee, N. H. it is known that he settled on what is called Fogg's Ridge, in Ossipee,' in 1798, going there from Hampton.   He was the son of Seth, the son of Abner, the son of Seth, the son of Samuel the 1st, by Mary Page, his second wife

Dea. Seth Fogg married Elisabeth Mordough, daughter of Nathan Mordough, of Greenland, now No Wakefield. Nathan Mordough was an educated Irish gentleman ; and it was from him that the daughter Elisabeth derived a so-called *grand air* or *grand way*, that made her person-ality a vigorous tradition to her descendants, for grace, dignity and superb mien in every respect.

The records of Greenland are replete with the name of Nathan Mordough, as an important man in town affairs. The same is true of his son-in-law, Dea. Seth Fogg.   ,

It was at Dea. Seth Fogg's residence on the Ridge, that the first meeting of the Baptists in Ossipee was held   He was a man universally beloved, and in very truth the big man of the locality, being credited with extraordinary powers of justice, wisdom and kindness.

In the Fogg burial ground on the Ridge, rest the re-mains of this noble citizen and his truly royal spouse, the tombstones reading,—

 " Deacon Seth Fogg died Oct. 8, 1841 aged 75 years."

 " Elisabeth, wife of Deacon Seth Fogg, died Jan. 16, 1843, aged 75 years."

Dea. Seth had four sons,—Daniel, Nathan. James, and Amasa ; and four daughters,—Polly, Betsey, Anna and Leucadia   They married as follows :

Polly, the eldest, married John Marston ; Leucadia married Wingate Titcomb ; Betsey married John Scates, and are the grandparents of the writer, Anna, the young-

est, married William Dame ; Amasa married Patty
Hodgdon; Nathan married Abigail Scates ; Daniel married Sally Cole ; James married Hannah Hubbard.

Near Deacon Fogg, on the Ridge, lived his two brothers,—Simon and Abner.

In Memoriam.

Read by Mrs. W. A. Fogg, Malden, Mass. Prepared by
Mrs. Adna J. Fogg.

John Blake Fogg, born at Monmouth, Maine, Feb. 14,
1825, died Oct 31, 1905, was the son of Royal and Ruth
Blake Fogg, grandson of Rev Caleb 5, (Seth 4, Seth 3,
Seth 2, Samuel 1,) Fogg, of Monmouth.

Mr. Fogg was thrice married : his last wife died Nov.
10, 1904 He was the youngest child of Royal Fogg, and
had spent most of his long and useful life in Monmouth

Nearly sixty years ago, he was one of the Postmasters
in town. Through his efforts the Post Office at North
Monmouth, over which he had charge, was established.

He was one of the twelve organizers of the Union Church
in that village.

In 1876, he joined the Maine Conference, and preached
in New Portland Vineyard, North Augusta, Lisbon, and
many times at the M. E. Church, at Monmouth Center

For nearly a dozen years Mr. Fogg was a Selectman of
the town. He was a Representative to the Legislature ;
and probably presided over the Annual Town Meetings
more successive years, than any man in the state in similar
office. For forty years, with two exceptions, he served as
Moderator.

Of the charter members of Monmouth Lodge, No 110,
F. & A. Masons, Mr. Fogg was the last surviving member.
He was the first Secretary of the Lodge ; and as Chaplain,
had been longer in office than any officer.

As an interesting speaker, he was often heard in gath-
erings of the town. ' His kind, sympathetic nature, and
impressive personality, have soothed the sick, and given
new strength to those in sorrow.

Mr. Fogg was a self-made man; and won an enviable
position in the town. At the reunions of the Monmouth

Academy, he has been one of the prominent alumni ; and
his reminiscences were always listened to with pleasure.
Cheerful and optimistic, he was a very congenial person
to meet

At three of our Reunions, he was present The last
occasion of our meeting with him, was in Portland, 1904,
when he was President of the Fogg Family Association.—
It was his intention to join us last year in Boston ; but
owing to ill health he was prevented, and, gradually failing, passed away in October, less than a year after his
wife's death.   Through his illness, much attention was
shown him by the town's people

Those of you who were fortunate in meeting with Mr.
Fogg, will recall his pleasant, cheerful greetings and the
smiling countenance.

Died in South Boston, Sept 8. 1905, Mary Griselda,
widow of Dr. John Samuel Hill Fogg, and daughter of the
late Rev. Dr. Joseph E. Clinch. Mrs Fogg was born in
South Boston, April 2, 1840, and married Dr Fogg in
1870. Soon after, he was stricken with paralysis. He
lived until 1893. She was a woman of fine training, and
rare intellect.

Mr. Fogg had a collection of Autographs which is among
the most famous in the country. By Dr. Fogg's will, this
collection upon his wife's death will now go to the Maine
Historical Society.   His library, which contains many
rare reference books, goes to the town of Eliot, Me. where
the Dr was born.

His will also provides for a Library, to be built there on
the homestead of his ancestor, Daniel Fogg 2.

Rebekah Dyer (Blake) Fogg, was born in Bridgton,
Maine, May 19, 1812 , died in Nashua, N H May 14,
1906 Her husband, Charles Snowman Fogg, was of the
seventh generation through Daniel 2, son of Samuel 1.

On the 19th of May she would have been 94 years old,
and without doubt was the oldest woman in Nashua

Born about the time of the War of 1812, she distinctly
remembered hearing her parents talk of it at its close.

For forty-four years since the death of her husband, she

had made her home with her three daughters, Mrs. George F. Shedd, of Nashua, Mrs Daniel F. Shedd, of Haverhill, Mass and Mrs John H Ayres, of East Boston. Three daughters, six grandchildren, seventeen great-grandchildren survive her.

She took a keen interest in public affairs ; and at one time knew by name every member of both branches of Congress.

She was a member of the Congregational Church, at Rolinsford, N. H. and her body was taken to that town for burial.

Miss Elisabeth Fogg, born at Pomfret, Conn. Dec. 8, 1838, died at Brooklyn, Conn Oct. 31, 1905 ; was the daughter of Edward and Caroline Mary Putnam Fogg, and grandaughter of Rev. Daniel Fogg 4, and the sixth generation from Samuel 1, through his son Seth

Miss Fogg was preparing a paper for our Reunion in 1905, on her grandfather, Daniel Fogg, for 43 years Pastor of Trinity church, Pomfret, Ct. but owing to ill health was compelled to lay down the pen

Catherine Buxton Fogg, born at Yarmouth, Maine, Nov. 8, 1822, died at Dorchester, Mass. Nov. 10, 1905. She was the widow of Robinson Fogg. Those of you here today who gathered at our 1st reunion, will recall an elderly lady, who was present with her grandson, and three great-grandchildren,—representing the oldest and youngest present

Trueworthy Fogg, Jr., died at Lynn, Mass., June 19, 1906 He was handling a rifle in the woods, on the 18th inst , and was accidentally shot, the bullet passing thro' the body, then lodging in the base of the spine, causing most intense suffering. He was born in Lynn, June 7, 1890, fourth child of Trueworthy and Anna Maude Bickford Fogg, and the ninth generation from Samuel through his son Seth.

Died Feb. 27, 1906, in West Medford, Mass Mrs Elisabeth Nute. She was born in Gilmanton, N. H. March 11

1826, daughter of John Fogg Longee, and seventh generation from Samuel 1st, through his son Seth. Mrs. Nute
leaves four children: Mrs. T. H. Edgerly. Somerville,
Mass., Mrs. Frank U. Warner, and Miss Ida B. Nute of
West Medford, Mass., Arthur L. Nute, Salem.

George W. Fogg, of the *Military Order of the Loyal Legion*
Born at Portland, Maine, June 20, 1837, died in Tacoma,
Washington, April 10, 1906. Married at Quincy, Illinois.
Oct. 13, 1870, to Kati Varilla Dills.

He was educated in the common schools and at Hamden
Academy, Hamden, Maine, preparatory to entering Bow-
doin College; but the Civil War coming on, he enlisted
as a private in the Seventh Maine Infantry, Co. K, and
served in the Army of the Potomac for three years, and
re-enlisted and served till the close of the War in the First
Maine Veteran Volunteer Infantry,

He was promoted at sundry times, being mustered out at
the close of the War as First Lieut. He participated in
nearly all the great battles between Washington and
Richmond, in the campaigns under McClellan and other
leaders; was at the closing scenes under Grant.

Upon his return home at the close of the War, 1865, he
entered Harvard University Law School, and took his
degree He soon found his way to Quincy. Ill and entered
upon the practice of his profession. For a short time he
was Commandant of the Soldiers and Sailors Home, at
Quincy. Went to Tacoma, 1893

He was elected to membership in the Loyal Legion,
through the Commandery of Washington, March 17, 1897;
Registrar 1899; Senior Vice Commander, 1905

He is survived by his two daughters: Lillian K. and
Helen B. Fogg. And two brothers: Edward R. Fogg,
of Beatrice, Nebraska, and Charles S Fogg, Tacoma.

Will of Samuell ffogge,

Hampton, in ye County of Norfolk, N. H., ninth Day of January, 1671.

(The Will and Inventory read by Mrs. Adna J. Fagg.)

In ye name of God, amen. I Samuell ffogge, of Hampton, in ye County of Norfolk, being very weake & infirm in Body, butt of Sound Understanding & of a disposing Minde, doe make this my last Will & Testament as followeth .

I solemly committ my Soule unto Almighty God, ye father of Spiritts, & my weake & fraile Body unto ye Earth from whence it was taken, to bee buried in Such decent manner as my Executors, hereafter mentioned, shal appoint.

And for sch Estate ye Lord of his bounty hath bestowed upon mee in this World, my Will is as followeth :

1st. I give & bequeathe unto Mary, my Beloved Wyfe, during ye terme of her naturall Life as her Dowrie, ye one halfe of my Salt Marsh, wch lieth on this side of ye falls River, towards ye Town, ye wch was formerly ye marsh of Roger Shaw; and so much of ye five Acres in ye little Common, as will make up her thirds of all ye marsh in my possession

It. I give unto Mary, my Wyfe, for her use, ye One halfe of Eight acres of Planting land in ye East Field, viz. ye 4th wch lieth toward Wm. Sanborns land towards ye North, & soe much as will make up her Thirds, of ye opland at ye South End of my House Lott.

It. I give unto Mary my wyfe, ye West End of Dwelling house duering ye terme of her Widowhood, & no longer ; but if she shall remove her Dwelling from thence in ye time of her Widowhood, then ye whole house to bee lett, wth ye lands, by my Executo'es, untill my Eldest Sone shall come to the Age of Twenty One years. & then my Eldest Sone is to possess it, & pay unto Mary, my Wyfe, her third of ye rent

It. I give unto Mary, my Wyfe, two Cows, & ye white Roan Mare, wth houshold Stuff she brought into ye house wth her, or wth bedding, or other household stuff shee hath Els where, to bee & remayn to her & her Heirs forever.

It. I give & bequeath unto my Eldest Sone, Sam'll ffogge, ye other two thirds of Land, Marshes & Meadows & Commonage, ye wch He is to Enter upon & possess when He shall Come to ye Age of Twenty & One Years, but shall not have full power in Selling and disposing of his Estate without ye Consent of my Executors untill He shall come to ye Age of Twenty fower Years.

It. I give unto my Sone Sam'll ffogge, all my Housing & barne & out housing, ye wch He is to Enter upon and at ye Age of Twenty One Years, paying ye thirde of ye Rent of ye House to my Wife during ye Time of her Widowhood, & for my Stock of Cattle & other moveables and Tools and Implements of Husbandray not Otherways disposed of by this my last Will, they are to be inspected and renewed at ye Descression of my Executors, soe as this ye Stock may bee mayntained and not wasted and imbezeled untill my Sone shall come to ye Age of Twenty One Years, & then to bee & remayne to him att his Disposall paying the following Legasies .

It I give and bequeath unto my Sone Daniell ffogge ye Sum of fiveteen pound to bee payd by my Sone Sam'll ffogge, when Daniell shall Arive to ye Age of Twenty One Years.

It. I give unto my Daughter, Mary ffogge, One feather Bed, and One feather Bolster, and One pillow, and Two blankets , One of them a Red Blanket, and Two payer of Sheets wch were her Mothers.

It. To my Daughter Mary, One brass pan and 3 pewter platters, and some other pewter and Earthen Dishes, wch were her Mother's. and these Goods being prized to my Daughter Mary, my Sone Sam'll is to make up ye Sum of fiveteen pounds to Her, when shee shall come to ye Age of Twenty One Years, or at her marrage, wch shall happen first.

It I do give unto my Sone Daniell ffogge ye Other Third part of my Land, wch He is to Enter upon and pos-, sess at my Wyfes Decease, & with in One Year after, to pay pe sum of fiveteen pound back again unto my Sone Sam'll, if He hath received it before ye Land fall to Him.

It I give unto my Sone Daniell ffogge my Two new

pewter platters, & a pewter Bason.

It. I give to my Sone Sam'll ffogge my Two Tables & One Bedstead, & One great Chayer, & Three Chests, and one new green Rugg, and a Suite of Curtains, and One Fowling piece, & all the Rest of my House hold Stuffs I give and bequeath to Mary, my Wife, & to ye three Children I have by her.

It. I give unto my Sone Seath ffogge, ye Sum of six pounds, To bee payd to Him by my Sone Sam'll when He shall come to ye Age of Twenty One Years.

It. I give to my Son James ffogg ye Sum of Six pound, to bee payd when He shall come to ye Age of Twenty One Years, to bee payd by my Sone Sam'll.

It. I doe give unto my Youngest Daughter Hannah ffogge ye Sum of Six pounds to bee payd by my Sone Sam'll when Shee shall come to ye Age of Twenty One Years, & if her Mariage shall happen Sooner, then to bee payd at her Day of Mariage

And my Will is if my Eldest Son should be without Heirs of his own body, then his portion of Land to Desand to my next Sone; & if any of my other Children shall die without Issue, then their portion shall bee divided amongst ye reste of my Child'n yt shall survive.

And I doe by these presents Appoint my loving father-in-law, Deacon Robert Page, & loving Friends Willi. ffuller, & Nath'll Bacheller, to bee my lawfull Execut'rs to this my last Will and Testament to see yt ye same bee p'formed according to ye true intent & meaning hereof, & if God shall take Away any of them, yt if God permit, they shall have power and Liberty to make choice of whom shall supply in his or their place in point of Executorship; & I do appoint my loving Brother, Tho: Ward, & my loving friend, Sam'll Dalton, to bee as Overseers to this my Will, who have ye like power to make choice of supply in their place, in Case of Death or removeall.

And my Will is, if my Three Eldest Children shal bee setled by my Executors, viz. my Sone Sam'll & Daniell to Some good Trades wch they shall most desire, & to bee placed in Such Families as may bee for their Comfort &

Advantage both for Soule & body as much as can bee Attained ; and I appoint yt such Wareing Clothes as I shall
leave att my Death, shall bee inspect by my Execut'rs, to
fitt out my Two Sones, Sam'll & Daniell, to Service, & to
make such further supply as they in their Discretion shall
Judge meet.

And my Will is yt my Executors shall take Such Care
both in ye Time of my Wyfe's Widowhood & att all Times,
yt my Estate may be preserved, & yt ye Housings doe not
go to decay without reparation ; and yt ye fences & other
things, doe not suffer Strip & Wast in ye Time whilst it is
out of my Sonn's hands.

And my Will is Concerning my Daughter Mary bee disposed off to ye Tuition of my loving friends Wm ffuller &
frances his Wyfe, & if God should take away Goodwyfe
ffuller whilst my Daughter Mary is in her minority, I will
and committ her Tuition unto my Brother Benjamin Shaw,
& to Goodwife Balcheller.

& my Will is ye Housings & land & Stock of Cattle
and other moveables bee [regulated ?] by ye Discression
of my Executors, for ye subsistence of my Wyfe & my
Youngest Children, untill my Sone Sam'll shall arive to
ye Age of Twenty One Years, & to this I Affix my hand &
seale as my last Will, this ninth Day of January, 1671.

SAM'LL FFOGGE.

and his seale to it

Signed and sealed in ye presence of us,—

    Wm ffuller
    Sam'll Dalton.
    ffrance ffuller.

Entered ye 6th Oct'r, 1672.

This Will was Proved upon ye Oath of ye abov sd
witnesses, Wm. Fuller, Sam'll Dalton, ffrance ffuller,
before ye County Court held att Hampton, ye 8th, 8th m.
1672, as attest,   THO. BRADBURY, rec'd.

The Inventory. 1672.

A true inventorie of all ye howses, lands, goods & Chattels of Sam'll ffogge, of Hampton, late deceased ye 15 day of April, 1672.

	£	s	d
—— his dwelling house & all his out houses & his house lot and his commonage :	100	0	0
21 Acres meadow & marsh	40	0	0
3 acres pasture land	05	0	0
8 acres planting land	20	0	0
3 oxen	15	0	0
5 cows and 2 thre yeer olds	20	0	0
2 yeer olds and 3 sucking Calves	03	0	0
1 mare, 8 sheep, 2 lambs	09	0	0
9 swine	03	0	0
one feather bed and bolster	03	0	0
one green Rugg and two blankets	02	10	0
1 bedsted & Curtains & vallance & one old bed	03	0	0
two tables and three cheasts	02	0	0
two boxes	0	9	0
four chayes & wheels & other lumber	02	0	0
one bed and two blankets	01	0	0
one saddle & two pistalls & holster	01	0	0
one fowling pesce & Sword	01	5	0
3 potts, 2 skillets & dripping pan	02	0	0
1 brass kittell, 1 brass pan & skillet	01	10	0
11 dishes of pewter and other pewter	02	0	0
sheets and other linnen	04	0	0
his wareing clothes & hatts	05	0	0
ploughs, cheyns, and a case of bottles	02	0	0
1 bolster, 1 blanket, 3 pillows	01	10	0
1 Skarfe & old coverled	00	15	0

These goods were prized upon ye 3rd of May, 1672, by us,—

Thos : Marston.
Wm . Sanborn.

—Mary ffogge, and Willi. ffuller and Nath'el Batchelder

made oath to ye truth of this Inventorie, & when more
appears they will make it appear. —— in Court att
Hampton, Octo'er ye 8th, 1672, as attest,

Nath'l Saltonstall, &c.

———

Bert C. Doe, of Newfield, N. H. (the Sec. pro. tem.)
read the Report of Mrs. Adna J. Fogg, the Sec. and Treas.
—a Report that was unanimously received and accepted.

The Election of Officers followed ·

President .

George Orland Fogg, Boston.

Vice Presidents :

James Henry Fogg, Biddeford, Maine.
Frank Appleton Fogg, Laconia, N. H.
Channing Folsom, Newmarket, N. H.
George Fred Shedd, Nashua, N. H.

Secretary and Treasurer :

Mrs. Adna J. Fogg, Boston, Mass.

Executive Committee :

Henry Melville Fogg, Lowell, Mass.
Willis Allen Fogg, Malden Mass.
Mrs. E. A. R. Ayer, East Boston.
Channing Folsom, New Market, N. H.
George Osgood Kensington, N. H.
Dr. J. L. M. Willis, Eliot, Maine.
Mrs. John S. Fogg, Providence, R. I.
Mrs. Frank A. Fogg, Laconia, N. H.
Mrs. John D. Fogg, Berwick, Maine.
Mrs. Frank A. Fogg, Dorchester, Mass.
Mrs. Bell Hodgkins, Springfield, Mass.
Mrs. Charles E. Fogg, Auburndale, Mass.

Extemporaneous remarks by different members of the Association, closed the meeting.

The speakers were :

Chauncey Folsom, Newmarket, N. H.
George Fogg, Beverly, Mass.
George Osgood, Kensington, N. H.

and several others ; and each spoke interestingly and entertainingly.

Clarence S. Fogg, of Newburyport, Mass., again rendered a solo.

It was then announced that the next Reunion would be at Eliot, Maine, at the Old Home of Daniel Fogg 2, son of Samuel Fogg the 1st.

Read by Mrs. Adna J. Fogg.

At·Kensington Meeting=house.

Know all men by these presents, that I, James Fogg, of Deerfield, in the County of Rockingham, State of New Hampshire, yeoman, for and in consideration of the ˙sum of four pounds, ten shillings, to me in hand before the Delivery hereof, well and truly paid by Benja Prescott, of Kensington, in said County, yeoman : the receipt whereof I do hereby release, remiss, and forever Quit Claim unto the said Benja. Prescott his heirs and assigns. all my right, title, Estate, Interest, Property, Claim and Demand of, in and unto that pew in the meeting house in the Gallary, Numbered [14] and is the middle pew at the East end of sd meeting house ; To have and to hold the said remissed premises with all and every privilege thereto belonging to him the said Benja Prescott, his heirs and assigns forever

In witness whereof I have hereunto set my hand and seal, this Twenty-six day of May, A D 1794.

JAMES FOGG.

In presence of
    Moses Shaw
    Affa Shaw

James Fogg is great-great-grandfather of
    Adna James Fogg.

Fogg Family Association of America.

Sixth Reunion.

HELD AT ELIOT, MAINE, AUGUST 30, 1907.

Members of the Fogg Family assembled Friday August 30, in the WILLIAM FOGG LIBRARY, in the town of Eliot, Maine, on the estate where Daniel F gg (who was born in Hampton, N H 1666, and died in Kittery now Eliot, 1775,) settled.

The Library is situated on the highest part of the estate, is built of field stone from the walls of the home farm, erected in loving memory of WILLIAM FOGG, the gift of his son,—Dr. JOHN SAMUEL HILL FOGG,—to the town of Eliot; and to be maintained free forever.

After registration, and social intercourse of more than an hour, a basket picnic was partaken in the old house and home of William Fogg, and most thoroughly enjoyed.

The members were then invited by Dr J. L M Willis, to inspect the Fogg relics at his house, on the Fogg estate .—

The pewter,— once owned by our common ancestor, Samuel Fogg, who died in Hampton, N. H. 1672, was regarded with veneration ;

and the old Chair, over two hundred and thirty-five years old, elicited its share of admiration.

A short walk through the field, brought us to the old Fogg Cemetery, where lie the remains of Daniel Fogg and his wife Hannah.   One hundred and fifty years have glided by since' he was laid at rest   His good name has been esteemed and revered all these long years by his descendants, to whom his broad acres descended.   The present owner and occupant,—Dr John L. M   Willis,— in the sixth generation from Daniel, is proud, and justly so, of his ancestral home.

Returning to the Library, a hearty greeting of welcome was tendered the Association by Dr. Willis, giving the freedom of the Library, and cordially extending an invitation for any future meetings to be held there

Owing to the absence of the President, George O Fogg, Vice President George F. Shedd called the Meeting to order.

Minutes of the previous meeting, held at Hampton Beach, N. H August 31, 1906, and the financial standing of the Association, were read by the Secretary, Mrs A. J. Fogg, and approved as read   She reported,—   .

Balance on hand, September 1, 1906,	$41	45
Cash received to date, August 30, 1907,	24	50
Total	$65	95
Disbursments to date, Aug 30, 1907,	$48	52
Cash on hand, Aug. 30, 1907,	17	43

The Officers elected for the ensuing year, were—

PRESIDENT,—

    George Frederick Shedd, Nashua, N. H

VICE PRESIDENTS,

    John L. M. Willis, M D., Eliot, Maine.
    Willis Allen Fogg, Malden, Mass.
    Henry Melville Fogg, Lowell, Mass.
    Joseph H Dixon, Eliot, Maine

SECRETARY, and

TREASURER,

    Mrs A. J. Fogg, Boston, Mass.

EXECUTIVE COMMITTEE,

    Mrs G F Shedd, Nashua, N H.
    Frank A. Fogg, Laconia, N H.
    Adna J. Fogg, Boston, Mass.
    Mrs Charles E. Fogg, Auburndale, Mass.
    Henry M. Fogg, Lowell, Mass.
    Edgar Hackett, Laconia, N. H.
    Channing Folsom, Newmarket, N. H

Executive Committee, continued,—
    George Osgood, Kensington, N. H.
    Mrs. Mary E. McGillivary, Boston, Mass.
    Willis A. Fogg, Malden, Mass.
    Dr. J. L. M. Willis, Eliot, Maine.
    James O. Gowell, Berwick, Maine.

It was voted to hold our Seventh Annual Reunion at Canobie Lake, Salem Township, N. H. the last Thursday in August, 1908.

Mrs. George L Davenport, Cohasset, Mass. will prepare a paper for the occasion. Subject, *Our Soldiers ;* she earnestly requests all data relating to Soldiers and Sailors of the different Wars,—sent to her not later than June 1 1908.

The Secretary read letters of regrets and greetings from members of Maine, Ohio, New Hampshire, Virginia, Arigonia, Kansas, Rhode Island, Connecticut, Nebraska, Pennsylvania and Massachusetts.

A rising vote of thanks, with three cheers, were accorded Dr. Willis and his good wife, for their kindness and generosity to the Association.

The Officers of the Association were thanked for untiring efforts.

Dr Willis announced that the proceeds from the sale of the Fogg Pamphlet will be used exclusively for English researches

Obituary read by the Secretary. [See page 132.]

God be with us till we meet again.

Mrs. A. J. FOGG, *Secretary.*

Obituary.

MISS FANNIE AUGUSTA FOGG.

Died at Malden, Mass , of pneumonia, on Christmas day, 1906, Miss Fannie Augusta Fogg. She was born in Boston, January 30, 1854 , the daughter of Thomas Jefferson and Nancy Jane (Lennox) Fogg, and in the 8th generation from Samuel 1st, through his son Seth Her great-great-grandparents were Phineas and Lydia (Fogg) Fogg. Lydia Fogg was the daughter of Simon and Lydia (Gove) Fogg, and the grandaughter of Seth, the third son of Samuel 1st

Miss Fogg was a member of our Association , was much interested in its works and welfare ; and often expressed the desire to meet and mingle with the kinsmen She frequently called upon the Secretary for information of the progress of our Association.

She leaves a sister, Mrs. Arthur J Huntley, Malden, Mass , and a brother, Thomas Lennox Fogg, of the firm of Fogg & Coombs, Westbrooke, Me.

HIRAM H. FOGG, BANGOR, MAINE.

In the death of Hiram H Fogg, which occurred at his home, French street. [in the early days of 1907,] Bangor lost one of the oldest and best known residents.

Hiram H. Fogg, was born in South Berwick, Maine, Sept 5, 1824 : the son of Isaac and Susan (Hayes) Fogg. He was one of eight children,—four brothers, Joseph, Edmund, Hiram and Isaac ; the last of whom died when young ; and four sisters, Mary Jane, Eliza, Abbie and Mercy Ann , all of whom are deceased, except Abbie,—Mrs A M Close, of Minneapolis.

Hiram attended the schools of South Berwick , but when seventeen years old he went to Bangor and learned the carpenter's trade, under his brother, Joseph ; the firm name at that time being Fogg & Wiggin.

When he was twenty-six years of age, the California

gold discovery attracted him; and he went to the gold fields; he expected to mine, but found his trade,—as Carpenter,—was prolific; the wage scale was $16 for each week day, and $32 for Sundays.

He continued in California about five years, then returned to Bangor. He soon became associated with W. S Pattee,—the firm name being Fogg & Pattee; and the First Parish Church, in Broadway, is an example of his work and revision.

He was elected also as the Chief of the Fire Department.

He married Caroline Simpson of Hampden. They had two children : Herbert, of the firm of Tyler & Fogg, and a daughter who died in childhood Mrs Fogg died in a few years. He married Clara Simpson, sister of his first wife : she survives him

In 1866 Mr. Fogg went into partnership with John Dole, in the Mill business, on Front street ; the firm name being Dole & Fogg Mr. Fogg continued in this business until 1891 when he retired from active life

Shortly after his retirement, Mr. Fogg received a legacy of half a million dollars, by the will of Mrs. Fogg of New York, whose deceased husband was his cousin. From this bequest, Mr. Fogg built the attractive Library at Berwick, Maine, known as the *Fogg Memorial Library ;* and also the Fogg cottage at Goodwill Farm

Mr. Fogg was interested in the Bangor & Aroostook R R He was a Director and Stockholder in that Corporation , and also in its adjunct, the Aroostock Construction Company

In politics he was a notable figure in the Republican councils; and was honored by election to the City Government, and also Represented Bangor in the Legislature.

Mr Fogg was a member of the Tarratine Club ; also of the Madockswando Club.

He was prominent in the Masonic body, being a member of the Rising Virtue Lodge, Mount Moriah Royal Arch Chapter, St. John's Commandery and the Scottish Rites bodies

He was also one of the oldest and most prominent members of the Odd Fellows in Maine.

Although not a member of the First Congregational Church, he was a regular attendant, and devoted to its interests.

Besides his widow, Mrs Clara Fogg, he is survived by one son, Herbert, and a sister, Mrs A. M. Close, of Minneapolis.

DARWIN C. FOGG

Darwin C. Fogg died in Keene, N. H May 1, 1907, after an illness of several months, aged 69 years, 2 months and 22 days.

He was born at Hancock, N. H. Feb 10, 1838,—the seventh generation from Samuel Fogg the First, through his son Seth His great-grandfather was Lieut. Ebenezer Fogg, of Fogg's Corner, Seabrooke, N. H

Darwin lived at his father's farm, at Hancock, until he was twenty years old, receiving the common school education, and also three terms at the Normal School.

At the age of twenty years he began labor as a carpenter.

In 1863, he went to Keene, to work for S. P. Ruggles.

In 1865, he went to Boston, as a general Superintendent at the Institute of Technology, where he remained for ten years.

In 1875, he went again to Keene, and engaged in the grocery and real estate business.

Mr. Fogg is survived by wife and one son, Herbert Fogg, of West Keene, and one daughter, Mrs. Addie M. Sylvester, of Seattle, Washington.

He was a member of our Association, attending the First and Fourth Reunions, and interested in everything pertaining to the name.

—Continued next page

ALVIN H FOGG

Died at Rockland, Maine, August 6, 1907, Alvin H. Fogg ; born at Thomaston, Me May 2, 1831 ; son of Isaiah and Charlotte (Hall) Fogg, and the seventh generation from Samuel Fogg, the First, through his son Seth.

He leaves, to mourn his loss, two daughters, a brother at South Thomaston, Maine, and a sister at Seattle.

Mr Fogg was a member of our Association , was present at our Third and Fourth Reunions, and read a Paper at the latter . it is printed in the Fogg Family Reunions. It was his intention to meet with us at Eliot, but, like the rest of us, he could not foresee the morrows.

BIBLIOLIFE

Old Books Deserve a New Life
www.bibliolife.com

Did you know that you can get most of our titles in our trademark **EasyScript**™
print format? **EasyScript**™ provides readers with a larger than average
typeface, for a reading experience that's easier on the eyes.

Did you know that we have an ever-growing collection of books in
many languages?

Order online:
www.bibliolife.com/store

Or to exclusively browse our **EasyScript**™ collection:
www.bibliogrande.com

At BiblioLife, we aim to make knowledge more accessible by
making thousands of titles available to you – quickly and affordably.

Contact us:
BiblioLife
PO Box 21206
Charleston, SC 29413

CPSIA information can be obtained
at www.ICGtesting.com
Printed in the USA
LVHW082350091218
599853LV00018B/166/P